SIBERIAN PASSAGE

INNOKENTY P. TOLMACHOFF

SIBERIAN PASSAGE

*An Explorer's Search
into the
Russian Arctic*

New Brunswick

RUTGERS UNIVERSITY PRESS

1949

A Pathfinder Book Reprint Edition
Complete and Unabridged

Printed in the United States of America

ISBN: 979-8869056016

INTRODUCTION

ALTHOUGH the expedition which is described in this book took place forty years ago, nothing has been published on its work except a few preliminary official reports and technical papers in Russian. A detailed description in Russian was being prepared for publication when, in 1914, World War I broke out, and work with the Red Cross brought my scientific activities to an abrupt end. During the Russian Revolution and immediately thereafter, I was more concerned with political, social, and economic work than with the preparation for publication of a report on the expedition. My departure from Russia which followed in 1922 again delayed such activity.

At the present time the expedition has been apparently forgotten in Russia, and outside of Russia it was never well known. The events of the expedition are told in this book exactly as they happened and should be considered in the light of historical perspective. I have not attempted to bring up to date my account of the life of that part of Siberia through which I traveled, or of the political and economic position of the Russian and native populations. I lack the data which would permit me to make a correct judgment on the changes which have occurred, and I am rather doubtful whether it would be possible to secure a complete or unbiased record from contemporary Russia.

From the reports of present-day travelers through parts of Yakutsk Province, however, there is some indication of how life there now compares with that of the time of the expedition. Conditions of travel, these visitors find, are not very different from those existing forty years ago. In spite of the fact that Yakutsk Province, now known as Yakutya, has become an independent unit in the U. S. S. R., orders from Moscow are as important there today as those formerly issued from St. Petersburg. Governor, Ispravnik, Zasyedatel, and other former officials have been replaced by the president of the Yakutya and the different Soviet commissars. Soviets function in town and village, but the political and economic status quo of the population evidently does not differ much from that of former years. Automobiles run regularly between Irkutsk and the upper Lena River, but in a greater part of the region horses, reindeer, and dogs are still the only means of transportation. The same work is necessary to prepare means of transportation for an expedition, and the same mistakes and negligence of the local administration are possible after forty years. Although the whole administrative machine has changed its structure and appearance, it has been impossible to change the habits of nomads dependent for their life upon their reindeer, or of Yakuts still living under the same roof with their cows. Securing horses among them still requires special messengers, long journeys, and meetings of local Soviets.

Unlike the inhabitants of Yakutsk Province, the Chukchi have seen important changes in their political and economic position. The Soviet succeeded where the old Russian government failed. Chukchi have lost their former independence and are now at the same level as other Siberian natives in their political relation to Russia. Many of the changes may be traced to the greater development of sea communication through Bering Strait in the postwar period, and to the growing use of aircraft. No part of the country is now so isolated as it was before. Undoubtedly recent visitors to the Chukchi Peninsula do not feel as if they were traveling in a foreign country among people for whom orders of the Central Russian government or its local agents have no meaning.

Material culture has not changed so much. The Chukchi still live in their *yerangas* and *pologs*, as they have for generations. Reindeer Chukchi still depend on their herds. The Maritime Chukchi of today still depend chiefly on hunting sea animals, and their successful years alternate with lean ones which bring them close to starvation. In general, conditions of the Maritime Chukchi have undergone a more favorable alteration than those of the Reindeer Chukchi. By Soviet edict the former have stopped trading with Americans. They no longer have their American rifles and have been forced, therefore, to return to the old art of hunting with bow and spears, the use of which prehistoric instruments was almost forgotten. Even in the best trained hands, such weapons cannot compete with an American Winchester.

The character of the native Siberian has undergone very little change as a result of the Revolution. If this expedition were to be undertaken today, and an account of it written, the story would be similar to this record of a journey made forty years ago. Certain aspects of Russia's old regime reflected in this book color the story but do not affect its essential elements.

Contents

SIBERIAN PASSAGE

1

ORGANIZING THE EXPEDITION

ONE AFTERNOON in the autumn of 1908 the telephone rang in my office at the Geological Museum of the Russian Academy of Sciences in St. Petersburg. The call was from General Vilkitzki, Chief of the Russian Hydrographical Survey, and a good friend of mine.

"Come to my office at once, if you can. We have some very important business here," he said without introduction or explanation.

A few minutes later I was at the old Admiralty Building. In Vilkitzki's office I found his assistant, General Drijenco; the president of the Russian Geographical Society, General Shocalski; and the governor of the Yakutsk Province, Mr. Kraft, in whose plan, unfolded at this meeting, I was to be involved for more than a year.

Governor Kraft told me that he was very much concerned about the development of the northern part of his province and particularly interested in the utilization of the northern sea route for the benefit of that really desolate section of the country. The possibility of commercial navigation along the Arctic coast of Siberia west of Bering Strait was still a matter of speculation, and further investigation and study would have to be made before a final decision one way or another could be reached. If navigation was worth while from an economic standpoint, it would require the organization of certain shore services, the building of navigation signs, and coal depots. Auxiliary stations would be needed where, in the event of wrecks, crews could find provisions and medicaments, and could establish communication with the interior of the country. It was also true that navigation along the northeastern coast would be helped very much if conditions of ice could be observed at special shore stations and reported to passing ships.

All of these questions had been considered very carefully at Irkutsk and Yakutsk, but Governor Kraft and his associates were at a loss to organize such a coast service when so little was known about the Arctic shore of Yakutsk Province. As a result Kraft had decided to organize a special land expedition for the exploration of the Arctic shore of Siberia between the embouchure of the Lena River and Bering Strait. Such an expedition would not only contribute to settling the question of navigation, but would serve to indicate the most rational organization of the whole shore service.

"I have come now to St. Petersburg," said Governor Kraft, "to get governmental support for my plans and to procure the necessary funds. You were recommended to me as a good man to head the enterprise. Will you undertake it?"

In spite of the suddenness of the proposition, my interest and enthusiasm for the expedition brought my quick though not unconditional acceptance. I told Kraft that I would want to work quite independently of anybody, that I should want to be assured of full assistance from local administrations without any interference, and that I should want the selection or appointment of all members of the staff left entirely in my hands.

I noticed that the last condition did not particularly please Governor Kraft, but he knew, as I did, that the approval of the Russian Hydrographical Survey depended upon my acceptance, and without that approval, not a ruble could be expected from the government. A very capable man and a quick thinker, Governor Kraft's hesitation was so short as to be hardly noticeable. "All right," he said, "I accept your conditions."

Although it had all happened so quickly, the difficulties of such an expedition were immediately obvious, and there seemed far too little time to solve too many of them. One of these concerned animals for transportation. As was always the case with expeditions in the Arctic areas of Siberia, these animals had to come from the local population, most of whom were nomads. It was necessary to meet these nomads at certain points where they had their gatherings once or twice a year. Between these gatherings they wandered over tundra or *tiaga* where they could be located only by means of a special expedition. If they were to deliver animals to us, therefore, orders must be placed with them a long time ahead of our need. The brief three-month period before our contemplated departure for the north could not be devoted entirely to such preparation; there was also the problem of funds. The expedition would ultimately be financed by the government, but since money was not yet assigned, no orders could be placed officially and no immediate progress connected with expenses made. Governor Kraft promised me all his assistance as well as that of his local administrative subordinates, but even he could not make any move before the allotment of funds.

Briefly, my plans for the expedition were to leave St. Petersburg at the end of 1908 and to begin work on the north shore in February. A week's time would be spent in traveling by rail to Irkutsk, and over two weeks in traveling about two thousand miles by horse team between Irkutsk and Yakutsk. Two weeks more would bring us by reindeer and dog team to the shore of the Arctic Ocean, east of the Lena River, an added distance of about twelve hundred miles. I expected to have at least three months of good sledge road along the shore which, with the long spring days, would give plenty of time to examine the Arctic shore between the Lena and Koluima Rivers. All necessary preparations for summer travel east of the Koluima River were to be made during the spring.

In my calculations I did not take into consideration the unavoidable red tape, an evil of governmental enterprises in all countries and at all times. Better to say, I did not expect it to be so bad as it was. Governor Kraft, the Hydrographical Survey, and the Minister of Trade and Industry were enthusiastic about the expedition, and I expected them to do everything they could to move the matter as quickly as possible. My expectations, however, were not realized.

Not until more than a year later, on January 2, 1909,

was it possible to bring together in an official meeting the representatives of different government institutions interested in the expedition. I reported my plan, and it was approved immediately and unanimously. I brought to the attention of the assembly the fact that too much time already had been wasted and that the expedition could not be executed before the end of that year. As a result, the assembly decided that the expedition would cover only the part of the shore between the Koluima River and Bering Strait. They also decided to solicit necessary money from the Ten Million Fund. In pre-revolutionary Russia ten million rubles were assigned every year for the purpose of covering unexpected expenses not provided for in the budget. Every minister had the right to draw from this source in case of emergency.

On February 12, about the time when I expected to be already on the Arctic shore, the group assembled again. Their first report was the impossibility of procuring money from the Ten Million Fund—the expedition was impossible this year! And everybody knew very well that if the expedition could not materialize this year, it never would. I took the sheet of paper on which I had noted my plan and crossed it out with heavy black lines, feeling a bitter disappointment and at the same time a certain relief. I was tired of the way things had dragged out, tired of all the walking from one department to another at a time when I should have been traveling north, tired of telephones and fruitless conferences. At the Department of Trade and Industry people were saying "Tolmachoff is permanently hanging on our telephone wire!" I felt that every day of delay made the expedition a more risky enterprise. With further delay we would be forced to use all the summer time for travel and could not arrive at the Arctic coast before the working season. The only promise of the situation was a most ignominious end for the expedition, and I could sigh with relief as I reasoned that I had been spared this failure through lack of funds.

My relief, however, was short-lived. Suddenly the assembly raised the question again; they began to speak of how important it was that the expedition be made this year, that perhaps it would be possible in some way to procure money. They considered again my original plan and decided to investigate also the part of the Arctic shore west of the Koluima as far as the Lena River. As the season was already advanced, the expedition was to be split into two independent parties. On my shoulders was placed the responsibility for supplying both parties with instruments, camping paraphernalia, arms, and other equipment. All necessary funds would be assigned to me, and I would have to make the final cash report. I would also have to find the necessary people for the western party. Such an alteration of my original plan, unavoidable because of the delay, left me with the great responsibility of having to direct its work while the expedition itself was under way.

Fortunately I already had secured a dependable leader for the western party. In 1908 the Russian Academy of Sciences had sent an expedition into the part of Arctic Siberia east of the Lena River for the excavation of a mammoth carcass found there by natives. This expedition worked under the leadership of a geologist, K. A.

Vollossovitch, who had been in that area once before with Baron Toll's expedition in 1900. Vollossovitch returned from the 1908 journey while I was worrying about the new expedition. When the split into two parties was decided, I offered the subordinate leadership to him and he accepted immediately.

I found two assistants for Vollossovitch, the topographer Yudin and the astronomer Scvorzov, and gave him a free hand in everything else. The choice of this leader was so successful that the western party was thought of later as an independent expedition, although in reality it was part of the same expedition and, in general, followed my plan.

Money was all we needed now, and this time the members of the Department of Trade and Industry showed much more energy and ingenuity. Money was found through a bureaucratic trick, one that was performed with extreme skill: The expedition would be sent to Arctic Siberia in the interests of eventual commercial navigation. When such navigation began to operate, steamers would call at different ports on their way along the Arctic shore and pay tolls which in time would accumulate to a certain amount. This money, which eventually would be collected, should be advanced to finance our expedition. Many years have now passed since that time and though a number of steamers and schooners have visited the Koluima River, no ports have been constructed along the shore and not a ruble of toll collected.

For my party I invited the astronomer Weber and the topographer Kozhevnicov. I had met the latter in 1904 when he was a captain in the Russian Topographic Corps. He had neither training nor experience for the work ahead, and this, coupled with his tendency toward nervousness, made difficulties for him at first, but Kozhevnicov was a careful and an enthusiastic worker and he soon overcame these handicaps. The friendship that grew up between us during the expedition was of life-long duration.

In the meantime a third party was added to the expedition. The Hydrographical Survey found it necessary to investigate the entrance into the Koluima River and commissioned for the purpose the twenty-five-year-old hydrographer G. J. Syedov. He was a good man to have on the expedition. He could bear the discomforts of Arctic travel cheerfully, and I found him willing, while he was with our party, to share the worries which often were more troublesome to me than the rigors of the expedition. Syedov's party was sent as an independent expedition and only during the journey to his destination was he obliged to follow my instructions. He was at no time to interfere with the travel of our party.

On February 18 the question of funds was decided positively, but more than three full weeks passed before we received the cash. The last link in the chain of red tape was the signature of the Czar; as soon as this was secured we started the final preparations. Governor Kraft dictated two long telegrams which I sent, one to the Ispravnik (Chief of Police) at Sredne-Koluimsk, which ordered all preparations for the eastern party, and the other to the Ispravnik of the Verkhoyansk District with a corresponding order for the western (Vollossovitch) party. These were the first and the last orders sent to local authorities. The telegrams could be wired only as far as Yakutsk, and from this town they had to be sent to destination points by special messengers. As a matter of fact, at Sredne-Koluimsk the telegram arrived on the second of April, almost three weeks after it had been sent from St. Petersburg!

On March 13 the money was assigned and the expedition finally authorized, and on March 16 we left St. Petersburg. I do not know now how I was able to do all that was required of me during these three days. All orders were issued, all questions had to be answered and decided by me alone. In addition to these worries, I had family grievances. My departure followed two weeks after the birth of my son. A more unfavorable time for a wife to be left behind could scarcely be imagined, nor was it easy for me to leave her in anticipation of a separation that was to last a year or more.

2

AREA OF EXPLORATION

THE NORTHERN part of the Province of Yakutsk, for the benefit of which Governor Kraft had planned our expedition, extends along the shore of the Arctic Ocean from the Anabar River in the west toward Shelagski Cape in the east, a distance of about seventeen hundred miles. The Arctic shore between Chaun Bay and Bering Strait, a distance of about six hundred miles, did not belong to Yakutsk Province but was a part of Kamchatka Province. Both sections of the shore were, however, so closely connected geographically and for purposes of navigation that the eastern end of our explorations was fixed at Bering Strait. The whole area is crossed by a number of rivers flowing into the Arctic Ocean. Among them is the Lena, one of the largest rivers in the world. Second to the Lena is Koluima River, which certainly could be navigated a long distance up from its embouchure but upon which none other than native boats ever had plied.

The southern part of the area is covered with forest and the northern part belongs to the Tundra Belt. The population is extremely sparse. With an area of about twenty-three hundred thousand square miles, Yakutsk Province had less than three hundred thousand inhabitants, or an average of eight square miles for each person. The Russian population of the Yakutsk Province was less than twenty-six thousand, or less than 9 per cent of the total population of the province. In the northern area, a couple of thousand Russians lived in a number of settlements scattered along the rivers. The largest town, Sredne-Koluimsk, on the Koluima River, had about five hundred people.

Most numerous among the natives were the Yakuts, to whom belonged over two hundred and twenty thousand, or more than 80 per cent, of the population of Yakutsk Province. The Yakuts lived in permanent settlements, and were cattle and horse breeders so much devoted to their animals that the stalls of the cows and the living quarters of the house were often directly connected. They had reindeer, too, but, like the Russian reindeer owners, they left the care of their reindeer herds to hired hands, usually to poor Lamuts. The Yakuts were a very vigorous tribe and, particularly in the years just prior to 1909, slowly increased in number and spread over the territory of other nomadic tribes, many of whom were in the process of extinction or assimilation by their stronger neighbors.

Among the dying-out native tribes the most important were the Lamuts, geographically separated from the Tungus by name only. The number of Tungus in Yakutsk Province was about seventeen thousand, not quite 6 per cent of the total population. Two thousand of them were called Lamuts, among whom were a number of rich reindeer breeders possessing large herds of these animals and carrying on the typical life of nomads by depending in their seasonal travels more on the needs of their herds than on their own. The Lamuts had to their credit a special breed of reindeer, the largest and strongest representatives of this species in the world. These reindeer could be ridden deerback even by a rather heavy man. A great number of Lamuts, however, had lost their herds and possessed only a few animals, hardly enough to carry the meager possessions of their owners during their incessant wanderings; their main occupation was hunting. Others had lost all their reindeer and were forced to become sheep-herders, employed not only by their more prosperous tribesmen but also by Yakuts, Russians, and Reindeer Chukchi. It was these less prosperous Lamuts who were most threatened by extinction.

Hunting gave these natives their food supplies, skins for their clothes, and leather for their light transportable tents. Fur animals provided means of buying different commodities imported into the area, some luxuries not excluded. Furs were given in payment of taxes or tribute for a long time before being replaced by money. The Koluima Basin was particularly known for precious fox skins, and at times quite fabulous prices were paid when after long travel a skin reached an outside market.

The most precious skins were often not put on the market but sent as a personal gift to the Czar. The lucky hunter expected to get more this way for his prey than by selling it to Russian traders, in most cases his pitiless creditors. The Russian priest at Sredne-Koluimsk showed me a very interesting letter on an old and rather poor-looking paper, signed by the Russian Czar Paul (assassinated in 1801) with the Imperial seal. In this letter the Czar expressed his appreciation to a certain Yucaguir for the skin of a black fox presented to him. I did not learn if the Yucaguir had received something for his gift in addition to this letter, but the letter itself was highly appreciated and kept in the family for generations.

Most pathetic was the fate of the Yucaguirs, who lived along the Koluima River; they had seen their good days but now they lived from hand to mouth in a worse state than any other tribe. Several months of starvation during a year had become an almost expected part of their routine. We saw only a few representatives, and these were not of the pure type. The whole tribe consisted of little more than a thousand people; their final extinction or assimilation by other tribes was only a matter of time. A similar fate has befallen other native tribes of northeastern Siberia; only their names remind one of their former existence. The main and almost the only occupations of Yucaguirs were fishing and hunting. These industries taken alone were not sufficient to procure under the existing conditions an independent and secure living. The tragic position of Yucaguirs and wandering Lamuts found at least part of its explanation in their almost exclusive dependence on those two industries.

Different from the position of these and other Siberian natives was that of the Chukchi among whom we carried on our work. Although the conquerors of Siberia on their eastward march had met resistance from various tribes, the overpowering of them had, in general, not given Russia very much trouble. The sole exception was the Chukchi. Nowhere in Siberia were fights between Russian invaders and the natives more sanguinary and less decisive than on the Chukchi Peninsula. As a matter of fact, the Chukchi were never overpowered by arms and were never forced to pay tribute. After many years of unsuccessful struggle, the Russians left them alone. The conditions established between the two parties could be perhaps better compared with an armistice than with a peace treaty. The Russian administration did not like to mix into the inner life of the peninsula and in the eyes of Chukchi they had no authority. The Chukchi had no official representatives with whom Russian authorities could communicate in any way; each Chukchi had to be handled as a separate and independent individual. A Russian traveler in Chukchi territory might well feel that he was in a country with a primitive population which was quite cognizant of its independence.

The number of Chukchi living in the Yakut Province west of the Koluima River was estimated at over fifteen hundred, and they were reindeer breeders exclusively. The number of Chukchi living east of the Koluima River in the Chukchi Peninsula might be ten thousand, might be twenty thousand, for under the political conditions of this tribe, statistics at best were only approximations.

The Chukchi were divided into two groups: so-called Reindeer Chukchi and Maritime or Sedentary Chukchi. The first were owners of large herds of reindeer numbering many thousands of animals. We met them west of Chaun Bay along the coast, where they came during the summer months from the inner part of the peninsula, the regular area of their wandering. Many of them had apparently never happened to meet with Russians or Americans and had preserved their patriarchal pastoral customs. The second group, the Maritime Chukchi, were permanently settled along the coast east of Chaun Bay. According to the views of some explorers, they originated from the Reindeer Chukchi who had lost their herds. Such an evolution or transformation was quite possible, but if so, it was a matter of a long time. In the eighteenth century travelers had found them where they were at the time of the expedition, practically with the same way of life. Their folklore reflected conditions of by-gone days surprisingly similar to the twentieth century. They have become wonderfully adapted to the coastal conditions of living, and such adaptation undoubtedly takes a long time.

At the time of the expedition, Maritime Chukchi hunted big animals with American rifles, although they also had various harpoons ingeniously made of walrus ivory; spears and other native arms were very little used. As animals of transportation, Maritime Chukchi used dogs (the name Dog Chukchi sometimes was applied to them), which again indicated a long period of adaption.

For their livelihood Maritime Chukchi depended chiefly on sea animals, such as seals and walrus. Land animals, fish, birds, and reindeer meat bought from Reindeer Chukchi greatly improved their diet but did not represent as staple a food as did sea animals. Although seals and walrus continued to be abundant in the sea, favorable conditions for hunting them were sometimes lacking, which resulted in an immediate shortage of food for people and their dogs alike. I understood that such unfavorable conditions depended chiefly on the conditions of ice and its distribution during the autumn period. At one time whales were also very numerous in the eastern part of the Arctic Ocean, but they were almost exterminated by American whalers during the middle and second half of the last century. When whales were abundant and the whaling industry profitable, many American ships entered the Arctic Ocean every summer, but only a few of them tried to sail far westward, the others for the most part cruising north of Bering Strait. The whalers carried on a small, incidental trade with Chukchi. When whalers could no longer be seen here, their places were taken by American traders who arrived in small gasoline schooners for regular trade with Chukchi living along the Arctic coast west of Dezhnev Cape. A few of those traders, more adventurous than the rest, tried to sail westward. Two or three years before our expedition an American schooner almost reached the Koluima, but was stopped by ice about a hundred miles east of Shelagski Cape, from which point the crew of three men arrived at Nijni-Koluimsk by dog team.

As a result of these visits of American traders the most eastern Maritime Chukchi, particularly those near Bering Strait, lived under much more favorable conditions than their western brothers. American trading schooners brought everything which the natives needed or which appealed to them. American manufactures and other products were moved westward again by means of winter dog transport, even reaching Russians on the Koluima River. Very often, in local language, American products lost their American origin. Such an expression as "a good Chukchi Winchester" I heard more than once on the Koluima River. The delivery of American commodities to the Russians was the work of individual Russian traders who happened to trade with Chukchi. As in the other parts of this region, means of transportation had a very small capacity here, and the Koluima District received very few American supplies from Maritime Chukchi.

Since almost all of the first settlers of the region were agents of the Central Russian Government, the work of supplying the Russian colonists with all the necessities of life was administrative. As a matter of fact, the government had not solved that problem satisfactorily during the almost three hundred years of its possession of the Arctic section of Yakutsk Province. A good example was the way in which relief was given the Koluima Cossacks. Although entitled to receive flour, cereals, tea, and sugar, they did not receive the actual products; instead they usually received their value in cash, with which they could buy very little, as the private merchant's stock of foodstuffs was always limited and kept chiefly for the more profitable trade with natives. The country did not produce any vegetable food. The Russians, therefore, like natives, turned chiefly to an animal diet. But while for the natives this diet was an adaptation which had been worked out from time immemorial, such foods were quite strange to Russians, who are rather inclined to favor a vegetarian diet. The main food of an average Russian peasant, particularly from the central part of European Russia, was bread, porridge made of buckwheat, barley, or other cereals, potatoes, and such vegetables as cabbage, turnips, or carrots. The Russian peasant very often did not see meat for weeks. Russians living in the north of the country, in the south, or in Siberia, consumed more meat and fish than their brothers of central Russia. But no Russian could imagine a good dinner without a hearty amount of bread, particularly rye bread. Besides food, Russians were in need of clothing, many different house paraphernalia, instruments, arms, ammunition, and many other things, all of which should have been delivered from the south, but which never came in sufficient amounts even with the assistance of the government. The failure of the government to meet its obligations may be traced to the vast distances separating distributing centers from sources of supply, the lack of ways of communication, and very insufficient means of transportation.

Southern Siberia could supply agricultural products for the northeast but was itself dependent upon European Russia for manufactures. Before the construction of the Trans-Siberian Railroad, which was not finished until the beginning of the present century, all commodities were delivered from Moscow or Nijni Novgorod to Irkutsk, the main center of distribution for all northeastern Siberia, by means of horse-team transport, which required more than a year's time. Even with the construction of the railroad it was necessary for materials to cover about three thousand miles before arriving at Irkutsk. From Irkutsk supplies were delivered to the sources of the Lena River, a distance of over a hundred miles, and from there on rafts, barges, and steamers down the river as far as the embouchure, a distance of several thousand miles. However, it was only the towns and other settlements located on the shores of the Lena River which received full benefit of river transport. Points inland, distant only a few scores of miles, in many cases could not get anything immediately because of the poor conditions of the land roads. As a matter of fact, there were only a few roads deserving this name available in summer, running from the river into the country and chiefly near the towns. Often it was preferable to wait for winter when every river, stream, lake, and swamp would be transformed into a good road for transportation by means of horse, reindeer, or dog teams. The winter road to Yakutsk, over two thousand miles long, was chiefly over the ice of the Lena River. It was used as a mail route and for individual travelers, as well as for heavy transport in an emergency, or when various commodities were delivered to the upper Lena too late for the short season of navigation. Yakutsk, which after Irkutsk is the second point of distribution for the northeastern part of Siberia, could be supplied by means of winter routes from the ports of the Okhotsk Sea, a distance of over five to seven hundred miles from different ports which are in turn more than a thousand miles distant from Vladivostok.

The huge Koluima basin had no benefit from water

transportation, and everything which was imported there was brought in winter from Yakutsk, a distance of about fifteen hundred miles, by means of horse and reindeer transport. The expense of transporting one pound over this distance was exactly a dime. In spite of the fact that the sources of the Koluima River are located rather close to the shores of the Okhotsk Sea, transportation in these areas required the organization of a special expedition, since for great distances there were no permanent settlements. All commodities reached Sredne-Koluimsk only once a year, and because of the backwardness of transportation the amounts thus received were never sufficient. Every year, therefore, before the eagerly awaited moment of arrival, there was a shortage of practically everything, and immediately after the arrival of the new supplies, abundance and wastage of everything. Such is human nature everywhere!

Some improvements in supplying the northern population with the necessities of life undoubtedly have been made during the time since the middle of the seventeenth century when Russians appeared on the Arctic shore of Yakutsk Province. All these improvements, however, were dependent more on the general development of economic conditions in Siberia and Yakutsk Province as a whole than upon any cardinal alteration of local conditions. Construction of the Trans-Siberian Railroad increased colonization of Siberia; the natural increase of the population in Yakutsk Province, at least in its southern part, moved the sources of supply more toward the north, but did not affect distribution in the northern area itself. A number of new roads planned within the most populated parts of the province would not have a great effect in the extreme north. Telegraph connection established between the cities of Yakutsk and Irkutsk during the last years of the past century, and the construction of wireless stations in the north during World War I, helped a great deal in directing transport but did not increase its capacity. Only the colonization of the northern areas, particularly along the routes of transportation, could offer such growth. The northern regions have been, however, too inhospitable to attract new settlers, and a natural increase, if it exists, is very slow. For regular supplies, horses, reindeer, and dogs were in 1909 the only means of transportation, as they were hundreds of years ago.

The sea route from Bering Strait into the embouchure of the Koluima River was never used commercially before our expedition, although in the opinion of many competent people it was considered quite possible. Cruising along the different parts of the coast was done repeatedly. Cossacks—conquerors of Siberia—sailed in their primitive vessels along the Arctic coast from one river to another. One of them even discovered Bering Strait and proved the separation of Asia from America without having any idea of the importance of his discovery. In later times the local Russian population turned from sea navigation completely, but different scientific expeditions cruised along the shores. Cook, for example, discovered North Cape in 1778. Nordenskiold had to his credit the first passage of the whole route along the European and Asiatic Arctic coast, which he accomplished in two seasons. Russian navy boats passed through Bering Strait into the Arctic Ocean at different times, although they did not sail far westward; the same was true of American whalers and trading schooners. Our expedition was organized entirely in the interest of this northern sea route. Immediately after our expedition, the Russian Volunteer Fleet established steamship connection with the Koluima River through Bering Strait, which developed into a more or less regular steamship line.

3

SIBERIAN EXPRESS

OUR EASTERN party left St. Petersburg on the sixteenth of March. With us were Scvorzov, the astronomer of the western party, and Syedov, the leader of the third party, with his assistant Jucov. I considered it very important that all three of the men who were to be engaged in astronomical work should make parallel observations as long as possible. We planned to make the first common observation at Irkutsk. Vollossovitch, the leader of the western party, was not quite through with his reports on his previous expedition and could not leave until the twentieth of March. For me it was the first proof of the unavoidable defects in the organization of our expedition, if I were in need of such proof. If I had been the leader of the eastern party only, I would not have worried about Vollossovitch at all, but could have rushed ahead to utilize every day of sledge road. Because of his delay in starting, we lost a week of traveling time at a crucial period.

In Moscow we changed our St. Petersburg train for the Siberian Express, a simple operation generally, but rather complicated in our case because of our unusually voluminous baggage. We could not trust the railroad officials, but had to check every piece of baggage brought from one train to another.

The Siberian Express was one of the best trains in Russia. For a small extra fare, a traveler saved between Moscow and Vladivostok about two days in comparison with the standard or the post trains. The distance between the cities was covered in about nine days. Since Moscow was the natural railroad center of Russia, conveniently connected by rail with the whole of Europe, and Vladivostok had a regular steamship connection with Japan, the Siberian Express from its earliest days became a train of international character. This circumstance was not surprising, because the journey between the main Japanese cities (Kobe, Tokyo, and Yokohama) and London took only fourteen days when crossing the continent by the Siberian Express. In response to demand, the railroad administration was always anxious to have people on the staff of this train who had some knowledge of languages other than Russian. All cars were sleepers and were divided into compartments; first-class compartments accommodated two passengers, while second-class compartments usually accommodated four people. In trains operated by the International Society of Sleeping Cars, first-class passengers had private washrooms. Both classes received the same service and had the same sleeping accommodations, although the difference in price between first and second class was rather large. A dining car was a part of the train at all times. Prices were not higher than in middle-quality Russian restaurants and the food was usually good. The dining car was always open and contained a piano; it was a usual gathering place for passengers between meals. Some trains included a bathroom; some even had a darkroom for photographers.

Traveling through European Russia we met mostly Russian people at the stations and felt we were in a genuinely Russian country. Beginning at the Volga, however, Asiatic peoples made their appearance: Tartars of Kazan on the Volga River itself, Bashkuirs further east. Names of stations east of the Volga often sounded strange to the Russian ear, being of Bashkuir origin. In western Siberia, Kirghizes were frequently seen at the stations, and near Irkutsk we were greeted by Buryats.

A week of travel in the comfortable compartment of the Siberian Express was a rest for me and a pleasure for all of us. As always on this Express, the crowd was international. French, German, and English were heard everywhere; there was even an Italian count traveling with his wife. The weather, excellent as always in Siberia at that time of the year, promised us no delay in the work of our astronomers. In our party of six men, only Kozhevnicov and I were old friends, all others were new acquaintances. But a week of travel, without any particular business to attend to, brought us all closely together. I wrote a number of overdue letters chiefly in connection with my institute business, and gave information and instructions to the people who were replacing me during my absence. I also finished the reading of the last proofs of my book which was in press, but to which I could not pay any attention before leaving.

I had traveled by rail to Siberia several times and was accustomed to the immense distances, to the scenery which one could observe from the window of his railroad car, to the life at the stations which changed noticeably as one proceeded eastward. Our astronomers, however, being both novices, traveled with wide-open eyes and often open mouths. For anyone who in a brief time wishes to get some idea of the immense area of Russia and the ways of her people, such a railroad trip as ours is warmly recommended. In 1897 I had had an opportunity to travel over Russia with an international group of geologists. Each of them had traveled a great deal in different parts of the world, but not one of them could conceal his astonishment when observing the dimensions of Russia.

Beginning at St. Petersburg the train ran through the forest area of European Russia. A traveler saw nothing but forests and forests, endlessly. The almost complete flatness of the region helped a great deal toward creating an impression of forest without limit. The greater part of European Russia belongs to the largest and most perfect plain of the world. Differences of elevation which the train crossed between St. Petersburg and Moscow a railroad traveler hardly noticed. These elevations have no connection with the geological structure of the area but originate as the result of erosion by rivers or, speaking generally, by land waters. From the geological or physicogeographical point of view, this lowland of European Russia represents a peneplain worn down almost to complete maturity.

Towns and villages in that part of the country were

mostly built of wood, and wood was used almost exclusively as fuel. Even railroad engines were run with firewood. To see large piles of firewood at stations seemed rather peculiar to travelers coming from countries where coal was the fuel of railroads. The engine funnels had special spark catchers on the upper end to protect forests from fire.

South and southeast of Moscow, forests gradually gave way to steppes. The forest here lost the continuity of the north and near the Volga River was completely replaced by steppes. Wheat fields and grain elevators, which the traveler could see at every station, reminded him that he was traveling through the granary of Russia. At the same time, dry-looking steppes in many places, similar to the great plains of North America, reminded him of another fact, that this part of Russia might be very rich so far as its soil was concerned; in truth, however, it often was affected by terrible droughts, when all crops failed and suffering spread over large areas of the country.

Our train crossed the Volga River over a long bridge in one of the most picturesque parts of its valley, where the river flows between white or yellowish limestone cliffs, not very high but often dropping almost vertically to the river. The largest river in Europe, the Volga is very imposing in its lower course. In my opinion it held the navigation record among all rivers which I had chanced to see in different countries, and I had seen many of them. In summer there were passenger steamers going both ways, tow-steamers with lines of barges often of tremendous dimensions, oil tankers, and large, slowly moving rafts delivering lumber from the upper forested basin to the lower steppe area where one saw trees only in gardens. On some of these rafts it was possible to see small, ready-made houses which would finally stand somewhere on the shore of the great river. What I never had a chance to see on the Volga, although I traveled up and down the river several times, were Volga boatmen, for the boatman industry there had been killed with the appearance of steamers. Human labor might be very cheap, but oil-driven tow boats were cheaper.

Beginning with the Volga region, one could see ranges of hills announcing the approach of the train to the Ural Mountains, the conventional boundary between Europe and Asia. For the most part, the Urals were covered with excellent forests which were well cared for—a condition in general not common to Russian forests. The Ural Mountains had no good mineral coal but were rich in ores, particularly in iron ores, which were smelted with charcoal. The high quality of the early Russian iron finds its explanation in that fact. The Ural Ridge is very old, geologically speaking, and a great part of the mountains has been removed by erosion. In the part crossed by the Siberian road, the highest peaks rise only to about five thousand feet. An admirer of natural beauty could not expect to find there the spectacular scenery of the Swiss Alps or the American Rockies, but the Urals compare well with the Harz in Germany and the Adirondacks in the United States. Wide valleys often occupied by large lakes, peaks suddenly shooting up several hundred feet, rocks rising above the highest trees and permitting a wide view over incredible accumulations of naked rocks in the wood—all have attractions very difficult to describe but equally difficult to forget if one is lucky enough to have seen them.

The line separating Europe and Asia followed the divide, but in many places a traveler could hardly notice that he was crossing such a divide. For his convenience, on a more northern old road was erected an obelisk, on the western side of which was written "Europe," on the eastern "Asia."

The Urals slope toward Siberia abruptly. I well remember standing with our group of geologists on the eastern rim of the range. Several hundred feet immediately beneath me stretched the Ob lowland, one of the largest lowlands of the world. Covered with numberless lakes and groups of trees, it ran toward the horizon and, as we knew, far beyond vision. It gave the impression of something endless.

The west Siberian lowland, or the Ob lowland, is entirely different from the plain of European Russia. With the exception of the extreme north and southeast, European Russia is comparatively an old land, leveled by continental erosion at work throughout many millions of years. Conversely, large areas of western Siberia were under sea water during the Tertiary Period. In its southern sections there existed quite recently, geologically speaking, very widespread but probably shallow lakes. This flatness of the west Siberian plain is, therefore, a primary character, the direct result of its depositional origin. In the section crossed by the railroad the plain was distinctive in its appearance; in all my experience I have not found any other area in the world comparable to it. Although its southern part was steppe-land, there were also many trees distributed throughout it, chiefly in scattered areas. In many cases such areas were composed exclusively of birch trees. For this reason, a part of the West Siberian steppe (the Baraba) was often called a birch steppe in Russian literature.

East of Omsk, the steppe began to retreat before the forest, and soon the train ran through the Siberian virgin forest usually known as *taiga*. Taiga was the name of the railroad junction connecting Tomsk with the main line by way of a branch road. The local name for the forest was *chern*, a derivative of the Russian word meaning black or dark, and quite appropriate for the *taiga* where the dark green conifers grew close to each other with plenty of dead wood below, and where many parts were swampy and few passable. In winter under snow the chern did not appear as obscure as in summer when no sun rays penetrated through the thick foliage and the ground under the trees was in dark shadow. The chern was both majestic and oppressive.

At Krasnoyarsk we crossed the majestic Yenisei River, one of the largest rivers in the world, and again, as crossing the Volga, I was sorry for my companions that our journey was in wintertime. The Yenisei marks a very noticeable change in scenery. With the exception of its upper valley and one or two other isolated places, the western shore of the river is low and belongs to the west Siberian lowland, while the eastern shore is everywhere steep and mountainous. East of the Yenisei for a long distance the train ran through the central Siberian plateau. This difference between the two shores of the river was so well marked that Siberian travelers of the eighteenth century used to say: "The real Siberia begins east of the Yenisei." Over this plateau we traveled to Irkutsk, where we arrived on the twenty-fourth of March.

Irkutsk, one of the first towns founded by Russians in Siberia, was built on the right shore of the Angara River, to which no citizen of Irkutsk referred otherwise than as "our beautiful Angara." My companions were deprived again of an opportunity to appreciate the majesty of swift flowing water, though perhaps the hummocked ice gave them some idea of the turbulent current of the river caused by the outflow of Lake Baikal only forty miles distant from Irkutsk. The Angara is so swift that for a distance of more than ten miles from the lake it does not freeze over in winter in spite of the Siberian cold.

Although built mostly of wood, Irkutsk had a great many brick houses, some of which were very fine. Many churches contributed to the beauty of the town. Viewed from the surrounding elevations, Irkutsk undoubtedly was one of the most picturesque towns of Siberia, or even of Russia. Unfortunately the streets of the town were unpaved, dirty after rain, muddy in spring, dusty in dry summer. The town had no modern water supply. Water drawn from wells or delivered in barrels from the river was surely an inadequate supply for a town which for a long time was considered and called the capital of Siberia.

The favorable geographical position of Irkutsk, almost

in the center of southern Siberia, its rôle as a connecting point between European Russia and northeastern Siberia and between northeastern Siberia and Transbaikalia and the Russian Far East, and its position on the caravan route to China, soon made Irkutsk the largest town in Siberia. Without even one industry worth boasting about, Irkutsk carried on considerable trade and had among its citizens a number of rich people, some of whom owed their wealth to the gold placers of the Lena region. For all that rich gold region Irkutsk was a very important base. Capitalists of Irkutsk, mostly self-made people, showed their generosity to their town, typical of self-made men of all countries. In Czarist Russia, Irkutsk had the best endowments for charitable and educational purposes. A theatre, a museum, different asylums, a hospital, and a great many schools were founded with private money. Irkutsk had several million rubles for the foundation of a technical college. Once, driving with Kozhevnicov across the town, I mentioned the wealth of Irkutsk in charitable and educational funds, and offered to count all the different institutions that had been founded with private money. I was surprised myself when the count amounted to something like fourteen institutions along this one road.

Three miles from Irkutsk was located the monastery of St. Innokenty, the patron of Siberia, with relics of this saint, who was so much revered in Siberia that in almost every family one son was baptized with his name. From the long list of saints of the Russian Church, only St. Nicholas might to a certain extent be considered in popularity a competitor of St. Innokenty. The latter name was, however, unused in European Russia, thus every Russian (including myself) with the first name of Innokenty may be assumed to be of Siberian birth or ancestry.

The first blow to the prominence of Irkutsk was given by the founding of the Siberian University in Tomsk. The construction of the Trans-Siberian railroad created new important towns or increased the importance of some of the older ones, but not of Irkutsk, which lost therefore its position as the metropolis of Siberia.

Leaving the train in Irkutsk, we found it necessary again to take care of our baggage. Something could easily be forgotten in the baggage car, forwarded somewhere between Irkutsk and Vladivostok, and lost to us. During the week of travel the train administration had learned everything about us. We were already personae gratae. I simply asked the chief of the express not to let the train leave before I informed him that our baggage was all in order.

In Irkutsk we stopped at the hotel, which became the headquarters of the expedition for about a week. Our astronomers started to work at once. As an observation station, we selected the quarters of the local Physical Observatory. Its director, my good friend Dr. Shostacovitch, did everything in his power to make their work as convenient and comfortable as possible. My days in Irkutsk were occupied by business routine connected with my position as head of an expedition, with official visits, receiving materials ordered from St. Petersburg, paying bills, issuing new orders, and arranging the most important business of our travel over the next link of our route between Irkutsk and Yakutsk.

4

OVER THE POST ROAD

TRAVEL from Irkutsk was of an entirely different character from travel in any other part of the world. The trail led over the Irkutsk–Yakutsk mail road, a route but a little less than two thousand miles in length. The main purpose of this road was to maintain mail connections between these two towns and, of course, all intermediate points. The mail road also was used for the travel of government officials and of private individuals. The horse carriages, drivers, houses for the travelers' rest and for change of horses (so-called stations) were provided by the local population under a contract made with the government.

Usually every road of this kind was supplied with a certain number of pairs of horses kept at every station; on the road which we were to follow from Irkutsk there were eight such pairs of horses. A pair did not necessarily mean two horses, sometimes there were three or four. Perhaps it would be more correct to say teams, but the word pair was used in that sense everywhere in Russia and was found even in official rules and regulations concerned with transportation. Payment from the government corresponded to the number of these "pairs" put on the road. For the payment received under provisions of contract, the contractor was obliged to carry the mail without any other remuneration. The exact amount of mail was never specified in the contract and as a matter of fact it hardly could be determined, so there were always reasons for misunderstandings. A contractor usually thought that the mail was larger than he had expected when making the contract and was convinced, therefore, that he was working for a loss.

All travelers over mail roads, government officials and private individuals alike, paid for a horse for a versta (a Russian measure of length almost equal to a kilometer or two-thirds of an English mile); he paid from one and a half to four and a half copecks (approximately one or two cents) for a specified minimum of two horses to be used even when a traveler was alone. Usually solitary travelers tried to find a companion with whom to share expenses. On the Irkutsk–Yakutsk road the highest rate was charged, four and a half copecks for a horse for a versta, which was a little less than seven copecks for a horse for a mile. This money was the contractor's, plus a few copecks for the lease of the carriage between two stations if the travelers did not have one of their own. The government collected from a traveler a tax of ten copecks for every horse used by him between two stations. It was also customary to tip drivers about twenty copecks at each station, and while tipping could be considered optional, neglect of this custom brought poor service, whereas generous tipping often saved a traveler much time.

Stations were separated from each other an average of fifteen miles, and were usually confined to towns or villages, but if the distance from one settlement to another was too great, a special station house was built between the two points. At the stations a traveler changed horses, driver, and carriage, if he did not have his own, and the changing of horses and the reloading of the baggage required much skill. Baggage of people traveling long distances was usually very bulky and cumbersome and carriages were never exactly the same size. There were no seats in the carriage and the traveler had to place himself as comfortably as possible on his suitcases, boxes, and bags.

The baggage was always so distributed that the traveler could recline wholly or partly. Some kind of mattresses, felts, or rugs and pillows were, therefore, an unavoidable part of luggage. If a traveler did not carry such sleeping paraphernalia, he supplied himself with straw at the stations. This precaution was especially necessary because traveling went on day and night, and all sleeping was done in the carriage. When he was packing his baggage in the carriage, a traveler was also preparing a bed which he would use, day in, day out, sometimes for several weeks. It must be done in such a way as to exclude every possibility of movement of individual pieces of baggage in the carriage, or otherwise on the rugged Siberian roads the traveler very soon found himself lying on bumps or falling into holes, and his repose turned into torture. Everybody, therefore, who expected to travel for any distance always tried to have his own carriage if he could afford one, not only for comfort, but also to save much time otherwise wasted in reloading.

At the station it was necessary to be registered and to pay for transportation. Registration consisted of a record of the destination and the time of leaving the station, and permitted travelers the control of the use of horses. According to law, average traveling had to proceed at a speed of about seven miles an hour. A good tip noticeably increased the speed, but any temporary defects of the road could also lower it considerably. Special government messengers had the right to require the greatest speed possible under given conditions. I remember a story about an officer-messenger who was sent from St. Petersburg to meet the Russian heir to the throne (later the last Russian Czar, Nicholas II), who traveled over Siberia in 1891. This messenger covered about three hundred miles each twenty-four hours over a period of several days, an ordeal that made it necessary to send him to an asylum for recovery. The reason for such haste was the appointment of the heir Nicholas to a higher army rank, and the officer was traveling eastward with Nicholas's brand new epaulets!

According to law, when such a messenger had arrived at his destination, he was obliged to make his official call immediately without changing his clothes, even though they were covered with road dust and dirt. During the same travels of the Russian heir, another messenger was sent from St. Petersburg. The officer arrived at a certain point toward which Nicholas was approaching. There was nothing for the officer to do but wait. Carefully he removed his uniform without cleaning it, took a bath, had dinner, and rested. When the news came that Nicholas was arriving, the officer again donned his dirty uniform, took his dusty bag with his message, and reported in the condition required by law.

After use by one party, horses would return to their home station at a foot-pace. Here they were fed and, after a certain time fixed by regulation, they could be put to work again. All the data could be checked conveniently in the registration book, which the station-master was obliged to open to anybody who wished to make such inquiry. It was often quite necessary to do this, because the number of pairs on certain mail roads were more likely to be too small than too large for the needs of that particular road. New government officials traveling to their posts, or expeditions such as ours, created a shortage. The mail was the first to be equipped with horses, always kept in readiness a few hours before it arrived. Horses were assigned to other travelers in the order of their arrival at certain stations, government officials first, then private individuals. The result was that everyone tried to travel day and night without stopping for rest as long as horses were ready at the stations.

If the question of horses were answered in the negative and a search through the registration book did not reveal any pair unassigned, often there was nothing to do but to rest at the station. Stations could not offer any conveniences beyond a warm room, but travelers brought their own sleeping paraphernalia, and even the floor was more comfortable than a carriage or a sledge. Local communities also supported a few pairs of horses used exclusively for the travel of government and local officials. For example, political exiles sent to, or returning from the north were ordinarily transported by local organizations. Such service was much less effective than the government's mail road organization, since horses usually were not waiting at the station, carriages and sledges were of lower quality, and registration was practically nonexistent. Still this service was a little cheaper and could be employed conveniently when mail stations were overcrowded, provided one had the right to use this kind of transportation. If it were impossible to procure horses from either of these two organizations and travelers did not like to stay at a certain station, there was no alternative but to use private horses, and that was possible only in towns or larger villages.

At the stations it was possible occasionally to buy bread, eggs, milk, or even a ready cooked dinner, but it was only a matter of luck and, as often, of favor. According to law, stations were required to give travelers only a samovar of boiling water; they preferred, therefore, to be independent of chance or the favor of stationmasters and to carry their own provisions. The staple food in winter was the so-called *pelmeny*, or small round meat pastries, which, when boiled in water for half an hour, made a very palatable mess. A portion of several dozen was accepted as a substantial meal for a healthy man with a good appetite. Inhabitants of Siberia were extremely fond of their *pelmeny*, which was considered in large extent a Siberian national dish, although it was of Chinese origin. The next course was soup, which in Russia was made in a great number of varieties. In winter, soup was carried in the form of frozen disks of different sizes. Indeed, bread, cakes, fowl, *pelmeny*, fish—all were transported in rock hard form, but it was not difficult to make these pieces of ice palatable on the top of the hot iron stoves which could be found almost at every station.

Winter travel by horse team required a generous supply of warm clothes. Even in the second half of March and in the beginning of April, we not infrequently experienced early morning temperatures of forty degrees below zero, and the temperature would have been much lower in the coldest of winter.

Travel between stations was made usually in two or three hours, but it was always possible to meet with some casualty. Deep fresh snow, storm, water on ice, and other Siberian weather phenomena often delayed the sledge journey. One needed to be prepared to stay outdoors many hours without danger of suffering from frost. Over the regular inside dress, often reinforced with some kind of sweater and woolen underwear (which was warmly recommended), one put on a light fur coat. On top of this one wore a *dokha*, a long loose coat of deer or dog fur with the hair of the skin turned outside; on the inside, the *dokha* might be lined with another fur. The feet were protected with felt or fur boats and with good woolen socks. Fur hat, scarf, and warm gloves usually made of fur completed the customary clothing of the well-dressed Siberian traveler. If, during the journey, something happened which required the help of a passenger, the latter must cast off his *dokha* to be able to move.

While lying in the sledge, the traveler covered himself with a heavy fur blanket. The sledge was constructed in the form of a deep box fixed on runners with plenty of room for baggage and sleeping equipment. The rear end of the sledge often was covered with a tent-like structure for protection against the wind. When it snowed, a curtain was fixed in front; in bitter cold or at night, such a curtain noticeably increased comfort.

In Irkutsk, I found that the road immediately north of the town was already impassable for sledges. There was nothing to do but to send the sledges forward almost empty and to leave Irkutsk in regular post carriages on wheels. Our expedition of eight people, together with voluminous luggage, required exactly all the transportation facilities available on the Irkutsk–Yakutsk Road. Although we were in the favorable position of government agents, we could not expect to travel conveniently together. Vollossovitch and Judin arrived at Irkutsk on the twenty-eighth of March and were sent ahead the next day. Later in the same day Syedov and Jucov left, and late in the evening the astronomers of both parties, Scvorzov and Weber, departed. The following day I left with Kozhevnicov.

The road from Irkutsk to the first station was very poor; there was no snow, but plenty of mud frozen during the night in alternate bumps and holes, which, along with the grooves from wheels, made traveling quite uncomfortable. North of the first station we came again to winter road. Only at noon under the bright Siberian spring sun was it rather warm, although temperatures were invariably below freezing. Dirty streets in villages and mud near station houses showed, however, that winter was already passing.

A few miles from Irkutsk we left the low shore of the

Angara River and ascended the high right side of its valley. The escarpment was so abrupt that ascent and descent became a difficult and unavoidably slow process —a very convenient place for highwaymen! I remember, from my childhood in Irkutsk, that the *Lenskaya Gora* (Lena Mountain), the local name for that part of the elevation, was considered a very dangerous spot where robberies were rather frequent. A modest cross erected at the side of the road showed that somebody had lost there not only his possessions, but also his life.

Shortly after ascending the plateau we reached typical steppes, which reminded me at once of the steppes of Transbaikalia, familiar to me from childhood. As we met there the same native tribe of Buryats (close relatives of Mongols) as in Transbaikalia, we might have thought that we were traveling somewhere on the southern side of the Baikal Lake rather than north of it. The steppe, however, did not stretch far, and when we arrived at the sources of the Lena River, less than two hundred miles from Irkutsk, we were again in the *taiga*.

In the beginning we had trouble about horses. On the same day that we left Irkutsk a rather heavy mail had been dispatched from there, and now mail from Yakutsk was approaching also. Traffic near towns, even in Siberia, is always heavier than at some distance from them. Once or twice we exercised our right to use the local community's horses, overtook the mail, and moved afterwards with no handicap except the natural one of soft fresh snow, through which we traveled almost at walking speed. Most of the time our road followed the valley of the Lena River, very often for many miles over the ice of the river. In such places in summer there was no road on the shore, and communication was only possible on the river itself.

Several times we traveled through *taryn*, or water on the ice, of the Lena River, and always with a loss of time. *Taryn* appears on Siberian rivers during the coldest period of winter. The freezing of the river bed and the thickening of ice on the river as the winter cold progresses cause the river to be pressed into too narrow a space, and, as a result, water is forced onto the surface of the ice, where it turns to slush. Progress over such slush depends on the amount of water and snow, the consistency of the mixture, and its depth. The greater the cold, the greater the quantity of water pressed out. Sometimes the slush becomes impassable for a regular horse team, in which case the driver must be sent on horseback to the next village in search of help while the passenger waits patiently or takes a good sleep. Warm clothes, blankets, and comfortable arrangement in sledges are particularly appreciated at such moments.

With the beginning of the sledge road in autumn, all the sledges followed the same path; the snow became more compact on the path than on the sides, where it remained more or less soft. This hardness of the path grew throughout the winter, and on open places it even became elevated, as the soft snow could be easily blown off the surface. After a while it became impossible to use the customary Russian horse team of two or three horses harnessed abreast so that one ran between two poles with the others at the sides, pulling the sledge or carriage by means of double ropes. Now we had our horses harnessed in a single line, one before the other. As before, one was between two shafts and the others pulled with ropes. Such harnessing is called in Siberia a goose, whereas the name *troika* is used for horses harnessed abreast.

There was always trouble when two sledges met on such a hard, high, narrow path. Usually post horses had the right of way. Local people did not object much to leaving the road and struggling in the soft snow. But even when the road was clear, it sometimes happened that a sledge slipped into soft snow, and in putting the sledge back onto the road all male travelers were expected to give a helping hand. Occasionally a sledge completely upset, and then the job became greater because of the baggage. There was, however, no physical danger in such sliding and even upsetting in snow, as the traveler was so well bundled in clothes that he would not have been injured had he been thrown onto concrete. Rather, there was fun in these small accidents which broke the monotony of traveling during the fifteen days in which we covered the distance between Irkutsk and Yakutsk.

A typical day began when we arrived at a station shortly after sunrise. Still drowsy, we entered the station house and ordered the samovar. The stationmaster immediately made a fire in an iron stove, while we removed the ice from our mustaches, which often were firmly frozen to our scarves. We dried our scarves and made quick, rather cursory ablutions. Some Siberian travelers omit this operation completely during long winter trips, because in their opinion water and soap make skin on the face and hands more sensitive to cold and increase the danger of frostbite. In the meantime, the samovar was ready, tea was made, and bread and other provisions had lost their rocky nature on the hot stove. After a quick, plain, but substantial breakfast we were ready to leave.

The administration of Irkutsk had sent ahead a notice of the expedition, and everywhere horses were brought and even harnessed by the time we were ready to leave. We traveled till lunchtime, when again the samovar was ordered, *pelmeny* boiled and devoured in great amounts along with other food, and we were off again. Late in the evening there was a stop for dinner or supper, always with samovar and tea as an unavoidable part of every meal. For delivering a samovar and dishes, the natives expected a fee. Twenty copecks were an average remuneration; twenty-five copecks were considered rather generous but fifteen copecks somewhat too thrifty. If we came to a station between meal stops, we lingered only for registration, payment, and to stretch our limbs after two or three hours of reclining. There was no other entertainment beyond inquiring of the stationmaster about approaching posts and their sizes, when the members of the expedition ahead of us had passed, and similar information.

For reading there was only the Bible, or rather the New Testament, for the Bible as a whole was not particularly popular in Russia; then "Rules and Regulations for the People Using Post Horses" and "Description of the Road in Both Directions from the Station." Stations were usually decorated with a large number of cheap pictures or clipped illustrations. In a corner with icons one saw portraits of some celebrated priests and bishops, and pictures dealing with such subjects as The Last

Judgment, Ages of a Human Life, Portraits of the Russian Czar, and Rulers of the World. Elsewhere in the room were pictures of battles, travels, and hunting scenes, portraits of beauties, and pictures of lighter subjects.

On stops during the night one of us was delegated to leave his sledge bed and make all arrangements with a stationmaster invariably half asleep. For two drowsy people to calculate exactly the value of a trip between two stations sometimes presented difficulties, particularly as distances were often in quarters and halves of a verst, with the price set at four and a half copecks for a horse for a verst. The postmasters very seldom had change, and it was necessary to carry along a bag of silver and another of coppers.

The valley of the Lena was unforgettably beautiful in many places. The river had cut deep into the Cambrian rocks of the Central Siberian Plateau, and in its upper course it was a mountainous stream squeezed into a deep defile. Cliffs rose on both sides with their rocks protruding among the trees often in fantastic towers, walls, and ruins; their dark red made a striking contrast to the green spruces and pines, and to the immaculate white snow. Further down where the Lena has been transformed into a majestic river, the rocks protruded into the river as picturesque promontories.

Just above Yakutsk the shores change their character. Here they suddenly become lower, without any large outcropping rocks—a change that marks a new geology. From Yakutsk, the Lena flows through the Upper Jurassic or Cretaceous continental strata composed of sandstones and conglomerates. The whole Lena area gradually becomes lower from the south toward the north, and near Yakutsk in the Yakutsk Lowland, which occupies the largest central part of the province, it reaches its lowest point.

Through its low position, flatness, and permanently frozen ground, the area has many unusual geological characteristics. The large rivers have very wide valleys with many small lakes and very steep slopes; small rivers are often in reality a line of lakes connected with short shallow channels. A so-called grass river flows over bottom covered with grass. Particularly typical are the great number of small lakes in the areas between rivers. A traveler unexpectedly comes across such lakes hidden within the forest. They all have steep but not high shores, and mostly are located in the holes caused by the caving in of the deeply frozen ground. Permanently frozen ground occupies the larger part of Siberia, but in the Yakutsk Province it is frozen more deeply than anywhere else, and the effect which the thawing of the ground produces on the surface is much greater. Permanently frozen ground, that only thaws in summer for a few feet, strikes the imagination as something horrible. In Yakutsk Province, however, it is beneficial. In dry, hot summers the thawing goes deeper and the moisture which rises toward the surface protects crops against drought.

Leaving the steppes at the sources of the Lena, we left also the Buryats and traveled among Russians, many of whom were employed in the mail route service. They settled along the river at points conveniently selected for their work. Approaching Yakutsk, we felt that we were leaving the Siberia of the Russians. Stations acquired Yakutsk names. Yakutsk-type dwellings with their open-fire stoves and windows of ice were seen everywhere. An invention of subarctic Siberia, ice plates of five to seven inches thick were shaped to the size of window openings and fixed in place with a putty substitute made of snow and water. Only a dim light passed through these windows, but Yakuts did not read or write to any extent, and the poor visibility gave them no annoyance. Every morning the housewife scratches hoar frost from the inside, and sooner or later during the long winter she scratches all the way through. A new ice plate, prepared in expectation of this accident, would then be installed immediately. In summer, the plate of ice was replaced by a more or less transparent animal membrane, usually the bladder or skin of fish. When I was a boy, I was told many times that ice was used in window openings because glass often cracked in the terrific cold of Yakutsk Province. It was more probable, however, that glass could not stand conditions of transportation and had plenty of occasion to be cracked before ever reaching the cold Yakutsk climate. The few specimens of glass window panes had so increased in price by the time they arrived in the Province that they were too expensive for the majority of the population.

More and more people on the road were Yakuts, and drivers very often were Yakuts, too. Russian people conversed with them in the native language. Travelers in the middle of the last century said that the Yakut language was spoken in the Russian society of a Yakutsk town, and compared that fact to the use of the French language among the educated people in capitals and large cities of European Russia. Governor Kraft, when appointed to his post in Yakutsk Province, considered it necessary to study the language. I found that the small command of the language which I possessed was sometimes of very great advantage.

Kozhevnicov and I were traveling a little faster than our friends ahead, and at Kirensk we found our astronomers and Syedov with his assistant. Every evening they lost about an hour working with the chronometers. At Kirensk, where there was an old astronomical point, they decided to make observations, and we passed them. They were a congenial group, all traveling for the first time in such conditions and enjoying the new experience immensely. Scvorzov had much fun with his thermos bottle when, at temperatures below frozen mercurium, he offered a glass of hot tea to a surprised driver. This feat always met with great admiration. Unfortunately the thermos bottle could not stand the violence of Siberian driving, even in a sledge, and soon lost its mysterious qualities.

Kozhevnicov and I arrived at Yakutsk on the thirteenth of April. Vollossovitch and Yudin were there a day before, and our astronomers and Syedov arrived with Jucov on the fifteenth of April.

5

YAKUTSK

YAKUTSK, like Irkutsk, is one of the oldest towns in Siberia and was founded more than three centuries ago. It, too, had seen its best days. Three hundred years ago the route into Siberia was more northerly than the one we took, and the most important towns were Tobolsk, Yenisseisk, and Yakutsk, with Yakutsk the administrative center for Eastern Siberia. Yakutsk never became a large town—at the time of our expedition its population hardly numbered ten thousand people—but in contrast with the large towns of Siberia, it had a well-expressed national trend. In spite of the fact that it was an administrative, industrial, and commercial center for a large province, less than half the total population were Russians, a great number of whom had not originally been connected with the town but were instead transients or newcomers. The larger part of the population was a homogeneous mass of Yakuts, deeply rooted not only in the town but in the country as well.

For a longer time than other Siberian outposts, Yakutsk preserved its character as a fortified town with a permanent garrison. One of its curiosities was the ruins of an

old fortification, the wall of which had formerly encircled the town. Skillfully constructed of strong wooden
beams, these ruins were interesting not only from an historical point of view but as an example of old Russian
wood architecture. Unfortunately the aborigines utilized
the wood of the fortification immediately after it had
been abandoned by the government. Governor Kraft did
his best to preserve for posterity what remained, but local
vandalism was too strong. Only remnants were left in
1909.

Another curiosity of Yakutsk was Shergin's Well, or
pit, which created for the town an international popularity. The permanently frozen ground made it impossible to supply the town with ground water, and the river
was too far distant to provide a supply. Shergin, a local
merchant, decided to make a deep well which would pass
through the frozen layer and reach unfrozen ground
water. With great difficulties he dug about three hundred and fifty feet, still in frozen ground, and then was
forced to abandon his work. Regularly as Shergin dug
he measured the temperature in the pit and sent his data
to the Russian Academy of Sciences. A special expedition visited the pit and checked his observations. Unfortunately Shergin's work was not finished, and a rare
opportunity to determine the limit of the frozen ground
was lost. Shergin's pit had wide advertisement in Russian
and foreign literature. Much speculation took place concerning the observations of temperature made by Shergin
himself as compared with those of Middendorff, who
was commissioned to Yakutsk by the Russian Academy
of Sciences. In Middendorff's opinion, the frozen ground

at Yakutsk went down more than five hundred feet. The question of water supply during our travel was no better settled than at Shergin's time. In summer, water was brought from the river; in winter ice, which the inhabitants of Yakutsk found easier to handle, was substituted. Of course, everywhere in the north travelers always saw, stored outside of houses, big slabs of ice which would later be carried into the home and there transformed into water.

Yakutsk had not much to distinguish it from other Russian towns of similar size. Its wooden houses were built around large courts, encircled by high fences with formidable gates. Shuttered windows were closed every night, not only for protection against cold but also against undesirable intruders. Its few brick houses were mostly administrative buildings or stores, and a number of churches dominated the skyline of the town. There was at that time no such luxury as a hotel. We found waiting for us a large house without much furniture, but affording at least a shelter where we could sleep, eat, and work.

Yakutsk was the last point on our road where the latitude and longitude could be determined by means of telegraph. It was, therefore, very important for us to make some determinations with our instruments and chronometers after their long travel in sledges, and to compare our determinations with those already existing. We spent several days on preparations for the trip ahead, for the weather was good and our astronomers worked without any hurry.

New sledges, which I had ordered by telegraph, had

arrived and were prepared for all eight members of the expedition. These sledges, or *nartas*, were constructed in an entirely different way from those in which we had traveled from Irkutsk. A light sledge, the *narta* was constructed for one passenger, with small space for luggage. It was built without iron except for the nails used in upholstering. All wooden parts were bound together with leather straps. Runners were wide and flat like skis without ironshoeing. The main characteristic of the *narta* was its elasticity. A traveler could hear the squeak of joints and could feel with his body how the *narta* bent one way and another in response to the unevenness of the road. After a while the traveler began to realize how resistant was such an apparently weak structure. The strength of my *narta* was tested in a rather peculiar way. I carried along fifteen hundred rubles in silver, which weighed about a hundred pounds. The money was packed in a leather bag marked "ammunition," which lay in the front of my *narta* under my feet. In spite of this load in its most sensitive part, the *narta* suffered very little.

As we found later, the living quarters and *nartas* were the only preparations which the Yakutsk administration had made for the expedition; nothing had been done to provide enough horses and reindeer, our most important need. Officials at Yakutsk had sent ahead a special messenger with telegrams from Governor Kraft, but they did not use this opportunity to make an official announcement of the expedition to the people along the road. Such negligence had a decided psychological effect on the people, who thus did not consider our journey important.

The eighteenth of April was mail day. I requested a postponement of the movement of the mail, which would occupy six *nartas*, and was assured that the mailman had received an order to give me the right of way if I should find the mail a handicap. Later I learned that this assurance was nothing more than a very ingenious lie. The expedition was almost ruined by the criminal negligence of the administration of Yakutsk. Unfortunately, Governor Kraft was still in St. Petersburg, and in his absence his assistants were independent, and were perhaps even working for our failure as a means of getting even with their boss, whom they knew to be interested in the expedition.

If we had arrived at Yakutsk earlier than we did, the red tape could not have harmed the expedition so seriously as it was harmed by the late season. During the last weeks of winter the traffic north of Yakutsk was heavier, as there were always some people who postponed their travel northward until the last moment. In Yakutsk, I learned for example, that the priest of Sredne-Koluimsk had left Yakutsk for his home immediately upon learning that our expedition had arrived. Similarly, two days after our arrival and coinciding with our need for every horse upon the road, the vice-governor sent four political exiles with three cossacks in ten *nartas* to Verkhoyansk. These men were part of a group of ten or twelve who had been exiled from European Russia to Verkhoyansk two or three years earlier. In the beginning of 1909 these exiles decided to escape. They planned to go toward the railroad, following the same road over which we expected to go. Somehow they had succeeded in getting reindeer and horses from the natives, and reached Yakutsk. A long time before, however, the Yakutsk administration had been informed of their escape, and the exiles could have been caught anywhere between Verkhoyansk and Yakutsk, if a special expedition had been sent out to meet them. Instead of this, it was decided simply to wait for their coming. When they arrived, probably jubilant, they were met on the outskirts of the town and conducted to prison, where they were incarcerated until the time of our arrival when, to our misfortune, the administration decided to rush them back to Verkhoyansk. Two days after the first party of four was sent back, another party was to have left, but I stopped that, telling the vice-governor that I would telegraph the General-Governor of Eastern Siberia if the Yakutsk administration would not do so.

It is quite possible that the escape of the exiles from Verkhoyansk was influenced by rumors of a similar adventure in the district of Turukhansk on the Yenisei River. In the autumn of 1908 a group of exiles living at Turukhansk decided to escape to America by following the northern route across the central part of Arctic Siberia between Dudina Village on the Yenisei River and Khatanga Village on the Khatanga. Further east the route followed the general direction of the Arctic coast, and anyone with a knowledge of local conditions in Arctic Siberia would know that such a plan would be a complete failure. But the exiles of Turukhansk must have been very badly informed about the nature of the difficulties confronting them. At the time they were apparently certain of success and acted with rashness and cruelty. They began with killings at Turukhansk, and bloodshed marked their passage east. In some way or other the Turukhansk exiles succeeded in arriving at Khatanga Village, where they were overtaken by a pursuing military party.

The events of this attempted escape concerned our expedition because of the measures undertaken by the Yakutsk administration to capture the exiles. Twenty soldiers under command of an officer were sent to Bulun Village on the Lena River to wait for the arrival of the exiles if they succeeded in proceeding that far east. The exiles, of course, never appeared, and before Easter the soldiers were back at Yakutsk. The travel in both directions of such detachments, using at least a double number of *nartas* in comparison with the number of soldiers, was an intolerable burden for the local population. Many people who had returned from the north reported that reindeer along the road were exhausted. We were not discouraged, however, hoping that the administration would take as much care of the scientific expedition as it had for the military one, for with the good will of the administration fresh reindeer could be easily collected among the natives.

Another undertaking of the administration in connection with the escaping exiles could have had tragic results for our expedition, and I do not yet understand clearly how it happened that our eastern party returned alive. All the natives along the Arctic coast of the Yakutsk territory were notified about the party of exiles traveling from the west. Exiles were branded as robbers and killers by the local people, which unfortunately was true. The natives were warned against giving the exiles any help, and were permitted and urged to kill them if an opportunity should arise. I was told later that the natives had selected a place of ambush on the road between the Lena and Koluima Rivers, where they were sure they would have a chance to destroy the whole party.

The same message and the same instruction to kill at sight was sent to the Chukchi east of the Koluima River. When the Turukhansk adventure ended, the administration of Yakutsk apparently forgot to repeal its order. In the area of Vollossovitch's party, the news of the Khatanga massacre and of the soldiers traveling from Yakutsk to Bulun and back spread among the people, and the orders from Yakutsk had been automatically repealed. It was different with the Chukchi living outside of the more traveled areas, where they were not visited every year by Russians. Very often during our journey along the Chukchi coast I was surprised that the natives were much afraid of our sudden appearance at their camps. Their fear was very apparent when we traveled west of Chaun Bay and came in contact with natives who had moved to the shore from the inner parts of the Chukchi Peninsula for the summer time. I had not noted fear among the Maritime Chukchi east of Chaun Bay. I learned later that even the Russian colony on Dezhnev Cape was not quite sure that we were not a band of escaping exiles when we appeared at their settlement. Undoubtedly our travel among the Chukchi was going on under very dangerous conditions about which we had no idea and therefore could not protect ourselves in any way. We might have been ambushed and destroyed before we had any understanding of what was going on. Even now I cannot understand why nobody among the Chukchi made use of the opportunity to obtain many attractive things from the expedition.

The time at Yakutsk was very unfavorable for our preparations for travel to the north. It was Easter, when every orthodox Russian takes a week's vacation and tries to use the time for eating and drinking—more for drinking than eating. Our official visits were always Easter calls. Everywhere, the first thing we saw was a large table covered with various cold foods and a row of bottles. Kissing the host three times was the beginning of a call. Then followed a good drink and some food, and only then was it possible to speak of business. Most of the local aristocracy were gathered at the club where a charity lottery was in process. Society ladies considered us their victims and insisted that we try our luck. The first prizes were a horse and a cow, and I always wondered what we would have done if we had been particularly favored by luck. Fortunately, our prizes were hair brushes, paper flowers, or ash trays. I remember one of the most attractive prizes, three dozen new ruble coins fixed on a cardboard in the form of a star.

By telegram from St. Petersburg I had ordered at Sredne-Koluimsk various goods to replace money in dealing with the Chukchi. According to Governor Kraft these goods would be there, but at Yakutsk nobody could tell me whether or not I would find them all at Sredne-Koluimsk. I was forced therefore to take from Yakutsk several hundred bricks of tea and a bag of tobacco. Another necessary item was several gallons of vodka, for although importation of alcoholic drinks into northern areas was illegal, Governor Kraft told me confidentially that without alcohol I would be unable to travel among Chukchi. All my travels through the territory of Yakutsk and as far east as Chaun Bay passed without this use of alcohol. Later when we met winter on Shelagski Cape, and travel to the east was possible only by dog teams rented from Chukchi, conditions changed at once. Natives fixed as the price for a *narta* so much tea, tobacco, skins of ice foxes, *and* so many bottles of vodka. They did not ask if we had any alcohol, but simply stated, as part of the barter, the requirement of so many bottles. As I expected, I was reported to the authorities as an importer of alcohol into a forbidden area. Not only prosecution but even investigation was stopped, however, by the order of the Secretary of Trade and Industry, who took into consideration all conditions under which the expedition must work.

Our purchases at Yakutsk gave us six *nartas* of luggage, exactly as much as we had brought from Irkutsk. Each of us, including the Cossacks, traveled in a separate *narta*. Three Cossacks, one for each party, were commissioned not for the protection of the expedition but to act as interpreters. Drivers also had separate *nartas*, each of them towing several of them linked together. In all, our caravan consisted of twenty *nartas*. Since Vollossovitch and Syedov were traveling in areas where money was accepted, their parties numbered only ten *nartas* each. Thus our combined parties left Yakutsk with forty *nartas*, which we had to take over the same road as far as Verkhoyansk, where Vollossovitch would turn directly north, and Syedov's party and mine would turn east. To accomplish all formalities and fulfill my obligation to the western party, I wrote instructions for Vollossovitch by which I transferred to him all my rights and duties to that party, emphasizing the fact that the two other members of his party were his subordinates and concluding with a brief reminder of the main purpose of our expedition. When he accepted the money for his party his manner was very unpleasant, as though he resented my leadership of both parties to that point. And, although my instructions included no details as to how he should work, he resented them so much that when the expedition was over he sent them back with the envelope still unopened.

During the night of April sixteenth our astronomers finished their observations, and next morning Vollossovitch's party left Yakutsk. My party left before dawn on April nineteenth and the following morning was fixed for the departure of Syedov with his assistant Jucov.

Before leaving I received the last telegram from my wife. It was a great comfort to learn that everything was well and that our boy was rapidly gaining weight. The next news about my family reached me a whole year later on my way home. It is my firm belief, however, that it is better for an explorer not to have any news about his dear ones but to have all of his attention directed toward the work at hand.

6

COSSACKS AND EXILES

THE FIRST station we reached after leaving Yakutsk was empty, and our Cossack had to bring the station-master in from a village about three miles distant. Only after long delay could we collect horses in surrounding villages. The Yakuts were very unwilling to help us, and we were involved in continuous arguments. I had not expected to encounter so many difficulties after all the assurances which had been given us at Yakutsk, and the further away, the worse the conditions. At Kharagatergin, eighty miles from Yakutsk, we found only six horses. I decided to leave my companions and try to overtake the post which was ahead of us. I took along our Cossack, a driver, and three *nartas* of baggage, expecting to be away from the caravan a few days only. As a matter of fact, we were not reunited until two months later.

Three days later and two hundred and seventeen miles from Yakutsk, at Seguen-Keli, I overtook the post, waiting for reindeer which had been taken by Vollossovitch. Six *nartas* of luggage and the Cossack of Vollossovitch's party were also there. Immediately I requested the postman to let my party pass, but met with a determined refusal. My reference to the promise given by the vice-governor had no effect. The postman told me that an unofficial conversation about the matter had taken place at Yakutsk, but he could not get a written order permitting him to delay the post. Without such an order he did not dare risk a stop of several days, especially at this time of the year when a few days' delay could result in one of several weeks because of the possible sudden thawing of snow, the breaking up of ice on lakes and rivers, and the complete spoiling of the road.

Although it was a bitter disappointment, I could neither blame the postman nor be angry with him. I decided, however, to make use of his official capacity and his familiarity with local conditions, people, and language as some support in the most important task now — organizing transportation for our caravan. When reindeer arrived, they were still too few to take care of the post and my caravan, small as it was, so I left all my baggage in care of Vollossovitch's Cossack and joined the post. Unfortunately I met with bitter disappointment again. The postman did not care to give any assistance, even the simple co-operation always existing among people traveling under the same conditions.

After a while he began to work directly against the expedition. When I required reindeer from a stationmaster, the postman said that station horses and reindeer could be used only for transportation of the mail, and that the expedition should be supplied with means of transportation collected among the natives. The postman tried his best to get rid of me, but could do so only two stations or eighty miles from Verkhoyansk. Several days we traveled together to our mutual displeasure, and I could not understand this animosity on the part of a government agent.

Apparently our expedition was not welcome in Yakutsk—it would be better to say in official circles—and agents of the administration, such as this postman, were keeping pace with their superiors. Whenever I talked about transportation for our caravan, I was confronted with remarks about a special messenger who traveled to prepare transportation for the soldiers sent to Bulun Village on the Lena River, and the lack of any such preparation in our case. The natives thought that our expedition was something unimportant—perhaps more a private enterprise than a government organization. They often showed an active hostility, and only very determined behavior on our part helped to check their insolence.

The further north, the worse our troubles. Spring was very close. The roads were gradually becoming bad and the natives less and less disposed to help. On the twenty-eighth of April, I arrived at Diring-Olom, eighty miles south of Verkhoyansk, where I was forced to stay for two days. Also stranded at this station were the four political exiles and three Cossacks of escort from Yakutsk, and during the next two days I had opportunity to observe both groups rather closely.

The Cossacks of Yakutsk were a very peculiar group. They were descendants of those great adventurers, the conquerors of Siberia, people of an enterprising spirit and very much above the average in intelligence and courage. The descendants of these conquerors had passed through a very marked retrogressive evolution, however, and were now in general below average. Such retrogression can be attributed to the influence of permanent support of the Cossacks by the government, without requiring or receiving from them corresponding service—a regular dole system which had developed corruption through many generations. In the first scores of years during the conquest of Siberia, the Cossacks were fighting constantly, and their support by the state was natural and unavoidable. But as time passed and as the natives became peaceful, the Cossacks were transformed into colonists no different from other settlers. Yet the Cossack still received his dole and existed without working from the time he was five years old. From birth to his fifth year, his dole was half that of an adult Cossack.

Some amusing situations developed through this system. An unmarried Cossack girl with two or three sons was considered a rich woman. She had a dowry, but she had no good reason to marry legally anyone but a Cossack, for if she did, her sons would lose their class position and their dole. This technicality, however, did not prevent her from living a normal family life, for throughout Russia, and especially in Siberia, people were not particular about distinguishing between legal and illegal marriage. I was told about a teacher at Sredne-Koluimsk who had been living with a Cossack girl for many years. Four sons were born to them, which made the family quite prosperous. A local official told me that there was always a sporting interest in a Cossack girl's pregnancy. Which would be born, a boy or a girl—dole and leisure or the necessity of working for herself and daughter?

In spite of their name, the Cossacks of Yakutsk had

nothing in common with the Russian army. In addition to their use as escorts, they were commissioned as messengers or as guides traveling with officials and expeditions such as ours. In serious affairs when a skirmish was a possibility, Cossacks were never used. Those at Diring-Olom guarded the prisoners and could have been disarmed at any moment the latter were so disposed.

With even greater interest than I observed the Cossacks at Diring-Olom, I noticed the political exiles. Having been born in Siberia, I was familiar with such exiles. My mother was a pupil of the exiled Decabrists, who, in December of 1824, decided to create a constitutional monarchy in Russia. All Decabrists belonged not only to the nobility but also to the upper strata of Russian aristocracy. Their rebellion failed miserably; some of them were executed and others sent to Siberia where they were simply worshipped by the local population. My mother always used to refer to Decabrists as people not only of great education, but also of sound morals. If I showed, for example, some intolerance in religious matters, my mother, a religious woman herself, would say, "Decabrists never would speak that way."

When I was a boy, our house at Irkutsk was visited often by political exiles on their way to the Provinces of Yakutsk or Transbaikalia. There were also many exiles living permanently at Irkutsk. Names of some of these people I met in books and articles dealing with the Russian Revolution. When, during the Kerenski Government, Mrs. Breshkovskaya acquired, under the name of the Grandmother of the Russian Revolution, an international notoriety, I realized that she was the woman to whom as a boy I brought money from my rich relatives. All the political exiles were people of high culture; some had been college trained and others had been dropped from universities on account of their revolutionary activities. Like Decabrists, almost every one of them brought some light into the country of their exile. Some became local explorers and scientists, often of international reputation.

In December of 1905, somewhere between Yakutsk and Kirensk I came across a party of political exiles returning from Sredne-Koluimsk. The majority surprised me with the primitiveness of their ideology and the readiness with which they were willing to put their ideas into practice without paying any attention to contemporary conditions, the general situation, or historical, ethnological, and religious backgrounds. Most of them had swallowed their lessons without mastication and hardly had digested them. When later I was talking about this meeting, I referred to them as privates of revolution. The presence of such "privates" was a clear proof that the revolution in Russia was spreading more and more, and was involving wider and different classes of people.

My impression of the Verkhoyansk exiles was rather vague. I could not discover in them any ideology. We did not even touch on political matters in our talks. Political crimes were often directed against property, not with the purpose of plain destruction, but with the very definite aim of finding money for revolutionary activity. Such robbery acquired the special name of expropriation. Some expropriators were working honestly for their party, but others did not forget their personal interests.

Undoubtedly there were expropriators who worked solely in their own interests and who could be called simply thieves. Sending regular highway robbers to Siberia under the title of political offenders was one way the government undermined the high reputation of the exiles. The Ispravnik at Verkhoyansk (Chief of Police of that district), for whom political exiles were people of high culture and morale, was very indignant that the last group sent to Verkhoyansk had been designated as political exiles. "I saw their papers and read the minutes of their trial. I do not understand why they have been called political prisoners. They are just plain highway robbers," he said to me when we were talking about the troubles which the expedition had with these exiles.

But I did not spend the entire two days conversing with the exiles. The situation concerning transportation for myself and the party behind me had become still more complicated. According to contract with the administration, the local population supplied stations with reindeer in winter, horses in summer. The official date for the change was the sixth of May. To our misfortune, an early spring was predicted, the advent of which would make the use of reindeer impossible before the official date to begin the use of horses. Contractors took reindeer from the stations with no intention, however, of bringing horses before the sixth of May. Since I could not expect to procure any means of transportation at post stations for at least a week, there was nothing to do but collect horses from the population, or in other words, to do the work which should have been done weeks before by the administration.

The first day of Diring-Olom, quite unsuccessfully I tried to find horses in near-by settlements. Fortunately, a single horse was available at the station, and on the second day I instructed my Cossack to look for horses over a wider area. I gave him a written commission, although I could hardly expect him to meet anyone able to read my writing. The most important part of this document was my mastic seal, fixing to the paper a small feather, the recognized sign of authority which could not be used by anyone but a government official. The feather was a reminder that the business which was considered in the document must be carried out with a speed comparable to the flight of a bird! In our situation the use of the seal was real irony, but it worked.

The Cossack found a Yakutsk elder who was willing to take us to Verkhoyansk. Besides the regular fee for horses used by me and my baggage, I had to pay for horses of the drivers and for drivers themselves. If this extortion were bad, it could grow still worse. According to the regulations commissioned Cossacks were transported free, but I had begun to pay for my Cossack's transportation soon after leaving Yakutsk. The greed of the Yakutsk elder increased when I decided to use his assistance in securing transportation for my party from Kharagatergin. He doubled at once the established fee, demanding nine copecks for a horse for a verst, or for a pair of reindeer. He explained blandly that four and a half were the legal fee for post horses north of Yakutsk, which he had to pay the owners of the horses, and the other four and a half copecks he expected to keep as his remuneration. This offer showed me that the local population found it quite acceptable to deliver horses or reindeer for the established fee and that the administration should have had no insurmountable handicaps in preparing means of transportation for the expedition, even this late in the season, if it had been willing to do so. With the assistance of the elder I succeeded in hiring several horses for my party. I promised as a premium some old army rifles, which, although highly appreciated by local hunters, were never on the market in sufficient numbers.

The exiles promised to give Kozhevnicov horses which had been collected for their party and said that they would remain several days more at Diring-Olom waiting for the next change of horses. They asked only that we supply them with provisions and I left for Kozhevnicov a letter about this matter. When he arrived he abundantly supplied them with everything that he had, but nevertheless the promise given me a few days before was broken. The responsibility for the broken promise lay chiefly with the escort of Cossacks. They probably did not want to stay a week or so at a station only eighty miles from Verkhoyansk, and when horses for their party arrived, the Cossacks refused to give them to Kozhevnicov. In some rather mysterious way the Cossacks had obtained drink and behaved in such a provoking way that Kozhevnicov thought they were dangerous. The Cossack of the expedition whom I had sent from Yakutsk with Vollossovitch's party and a part of our baggage, but who was traveling now with our caravan, was drunk on this occasion to such an extent that Kozhevnicov was unable to awaken him and left him behind. The fact that Kozhevnicov was an officer in uniform had no meaning

to the Cossacks and in the eyes of the exiles it was perhaps even an argument against him.

Before leaving Diring-Olom, I sent a letter to the
Ispravnik of the Verkhoyansk district asking him for
help, not so much for myself as for my companions
slowly moving somewhere behind with our heavy caravan. I had very little hope that this letter would be delivered to its destination. It was delivered, however, and
helped us a great deal.

Our baggage now had to be transported on horseback,
and we had much trouble with the horses during this
loading. Yakutsk horses are very wild. I think that in
comparison with other horses which I have observed and
used in different parts of the world, they are the wildest.
And after the long winter rest they were worse than
ever. The behavior of one horse was unexpectedly pleasing. We lassoed and threw it, and bound, saddled, and
loaded it with everything that was heavy, compact, and
unbreakable. In my estimation the load was not less than
three hundred pounds, almost double the weight of a
regular load. Then we took the ropes off. The horse
leaped wildly, but grew tame immediately. In spite of its
small size (horses of Yakutsk are practically ponies) and
apparent lack of force, that horse covered easily all
eighty miles to Verkhoyansk with its double load.

On the road three to five pack horses were usually
lined up so that the rein of one was bound to the tail of
another, and every bundle was in the charge of a separate
driver. For a while everything went well. But suddenly
one horse stumbled and pulled the tail of the horse in
front. The latter immediately kicked in the direction of

the supposed offender, which attacked the croup of the kicking horse with its teeth and simultaneously pulled its own tail. The horse behind now received a good kick, and the tale began all over again. Sometimes all the horses in a bundle became involved in a fight, and the driver had a job on his hands making peace among these wild animals. If some of the load slipped from the saddle, the chaos became still greater, for it usually scared a fighting horse terribly.

Early on the second of May I arrived at Verkhoyansk, having covered five hundred and eighty miles in thirteen days, an average of about forty-five miles per day. From Yakutsk our road had passed through the Yakutsk Lowland, often through dense forest where the snow was rather deep and the road narrow. More often, however, the forest was sparse, with large open places. Several stations from Yakutsk, the Verkhoyansk District began. Its border followed a divide between the sources of the Egiy River (the left tributary of the Yana River) and the source of the Kelya River (the right tributary of the Aldan River). The divide was so low and inconspicuous that the local administration found it necessary to erect a special sign on the frontier of the Verkhoyansk District. This road over the divide was new. On the old road, which had been abandoned not more than ten years before, it was necessary to cross the Verkhoyansk Ridge over a pass which had very steep slopes on both sides. The ascent was very difficult, and the descent was quite a problem. The pass was also characterized by extremely strong winds, although in general this part of the country is almost windless. During his first Siberian expedition in

1901, Vollossovitch had a rather amusing experience here. He left his *narta* and walked over the pass. It was very cold and he kept on his *dokha*, which made him very clumsy. When he reached the top of the pass, he met such a heavy blow that it took him off his feet and he rolled down, to the great amusement of his men.

North from the divide our road followed the valley of the Egiy River and then turned into the valley of the Yana River, which we followed to Verkhoyansk. The valley of the Egiy was very deep and bordered with high mountains. Several times we could see from our road the high, bared peaks of the Verkhoyansk Ridge. Under the peaks we saw so-called cirques or bowl-shaped valleys typical of mountains which formerly had been covered by glaciers. I thought that in the front of one of these cirques I saw small, irregular hills and piles of rocks covered with snow, in which I was ready to recognize a frontal moraine of a former glacier. The forest was rather poor, very sparse, with trees hardly large enough to be used for the construction of good houses. Open spaces were so wide that in places the area became steppe-like. There was very little snow on such open places; often the ground was even bare. I also saw here many burros which reminded me of susliks, a typical animal of the steppe.

7

A RETARDED SPRING

AT VERKHOYANSK I learned that my letter from Diring-Olom had been received and that preparations for our travel were going forward with great energy. The Ispravnik had left for the north to prepare what was necessary for Vollossovitch's party, and his assistant did everything for us. I did not expect, in spite of the energy shown by the Verkhoyansk administration, that horses would be ready for us immediately on the road and decided to wait for my companions at Verkhoyansk where I had considerable work to do.

The lowest temperature observed at Verkhoyansk was 93.6 degrees below zero Fahrenheit. As the maximum summer temperature was 93.6 degrees Fahrenheit, the difference between the two extremes was 187 degrees! But the dwellers at Verkhoyansk did not complain much of their climate; they enjoyed the hot summer, and did not find unbearable the coldest days of winter, because the climate was completely calm. Undoubtedly they were proud of their extreme cold, for because of it their miserable town with its less than five hundred inhabitants was internationally known.

After two days of my stay at Verkhoyansk, quite un-expectedly Syedov arrived with three *nartas* and one driver. He had brought along only his instruments, hav-ing left the rest of his baggage in the care of his Cossack-interpreter and his assistant, who did not arrive until the next day. I could not understand why Kozhevnicov had not used the horses taken by Syedov and Jucov for the transportation of at least a part of our caravan. Accord-ing to the plan worked out and approved in St. Peters-burg, we should have had the right of way in all cases. But I could not blame Syedov that under present condi-tions he had managed in some way to pass our party.

Later I learned that Kozhevnicov had arrived at Verkhoyansk so nervous and so near physical exhaustion that he had had to seek medical aid. The last few stations before Verkhoyansk were for them the most difficult on the whole road to Sredne-Koluimsk, in spite of the fact that my efforts and orders issued from Verkhoyansk helped them to some extent. At times the population re-sorted to nothing less than extortion. Once it was neces-sary for Kozhevnicov to hire special shepherds for a night, because the station people would not take care of the expedition reindeer. The caravan arrived at Verkhoyansk with pack horses and with reindeer and oxen harnessed to *nartas*.

The energy and self-confidence of my companions had suffered very much on account of all the handi-caps through which we had passed; they never re-captured the mood in which we had left St. Petersburg. In the frank report to General Selivanov, General-Governor of Eastern Siberia, which I wrote from

Verkhoyansk, I found a release from almost intolerable pressure. I told in detail about all our mishaps and the negligence of the administration at Yakutsk, and the outburst was better for me than any medical help. Much later, on my way home, I learned with certain satisfaction that General Selivanov had paid full attention to my report; he had reacted with the decision and austerity of the old soldier he was in punishing the negligence of everyone from Governor Kraft to the postman.

The arrival of Syedov's party changed my plans again. I could neither push ahead of him nor let him leave Verkhoyansk before me. I decided, therefore, to go with him instead of waiting any longer for my companions. I took all my baggage and Syedov his instruments, and with a Cossack, two drivers, and ten horses we moved onward. Jucov was ordered to wait at Verkhoyansk for Kozhevnicov and to leave with the latter, provided they had a sufficient number of horses. Otherwise Jucov was ordered to give Kozhevnicov the right of way and to follow him, having care of Syedov's baggage and also of all supplies which Kozhevnicov might leave along the way. I had recommended that, in case of emergency, he leave behind everything but the minimum equipment without which, in his opinion, we should not be able to do our work.

Riding saddle horses, we left Verkhoyansk the evening of the fourth of May. With the exception of Syedov's chronometers, our baggage was carried on horseback and my *narta* was used to convey instruments. Fifty to sixty miles a day was considered a great achievement with horses so heavily loaded.

We decided to proceed eastward as fast as possible, stopping only to feed the horses and to prepare food for ourselves. We managed to take short naps during such stops. In that way we covered over a hundred and eighty miles in three days. Traveling almost constantly, we always felt drowsy, and at times would suddenly fall asleep. But the saddle was not a bed and the loss of equilibrium awakened us immediately. I dreamed, mixing dream with reality. We were passing a number of wooden fences. I saw iron fences reminiscent of the one around the Summer Garden in St. Petersburg, a fence beautiful in the admirable simplicity of its design. Poor, low houses, dispersed behind these fences, were transformed into the great summer houses around St. Petersburg, into castles, into churches. And then we traveled through especially monotonous areas similar to the country near Verkhoyansk; there were extensive plains, scarce, rarefied and poor forest—vast open areas reminding one of steppes. Far away on the horizon the peaks of the Khas-Khaya-Ktakh Ridge helped to break the monotony of the landscape.

At the end of the third day we overtook natives with a number of horses sent ahead for our use by order from Verkhoyansk. That was as far eastward as the orders from Verkhoyansk had had time to reach. We were, therefore, not surprised that we found no horses at the next station and were indeed rather glad to stop for a while and rest. After a speedy supper, I made a few entries in my diary. "What an iron man you are, Mr. Tolmachoff!" called out Syedov in a sleepy voice. A few minutes later I also slept as though dead.

We had no idea where Kozhevnicov and Jucov were, but felt quite sure that through such a heroic three-day-passage we had left them far behind. Next day we procured horses and were again on our way. We were forced to leave my *narta* at the Tostakh station and to place the box with chronometers on a saddle. The tamest horse and a special attendant were selected for this delicate task. Spring was progressing. Beyond the station, water over the ice of the Tostakh River, which we had to cross, made the going slippery. One loaded horse fell and twelve dozen photographic plates in a soldered tin box were almost ruined. The soldering was defective but even so it proved better than none and we were able to use the plates.

On the Dogdo River we had much trouble with *taryn*, this time not because of spring warmth, as on the Lena River where the *taryn* covered only a limited area, but because of winter cold. The *taryn* of the Dogdo River covered wide areas, with water flowing out over the surface of ice throughout the winter and freezing very quickly, thus covering the valley with ice for many square miles.

Here and there a traveler over frozen lakes could see trees protruding above the ice, clearly indicating an island which had become flooded and frozen over. Day temperatures were comparatively high, and water, snow, and ice crystals made a gruel-like mixture through which we plodded mile after mile. At times the slushy, crystalline mass was encrusted with a sheet of ice. During the day the overlying sheet of ice was not strong, and when our horses broke through at a deep place, or where their hoofs, never shod, found smooth ice, our advance was extremely slow. Nights were still very cold and *taryns* became firmly frozen on the surface, making the river ice impassable for our caravan. We made detours along the steep slope of the valley, which was covered with forest, heavy underbrush, and snow. Very often we could not decide which road would be the easier, through the forest or over the ice of the river. No matter which we chose, we could move but slowly; in spite of the fact that we had horses, the passage to the following station, Usul-Kytyl, a distance of sixty-seven miles, took two and a half days. Although we saw much snow in the forest and underbrush, in general there was very little snow even within the valley; in many places there was not enough to cover the yellow grass of the previous summer. No wonder that horses in the Province of Yakutsk north of the Arctic Circle could be grassed in free throughout the year.

The weather in the meantime changed to the best for us and became much colder. The first days after we left Verkhoyansk had been rather warm, and on the eighth of May we saw the so-called snow mosquitoes and had rain the same evening, which, however, soon changed to snow. The temperature dropped noticeably; although this drop in temperature was due in part to the greater elevation of our road, it was also true that spring was retarded and the danger of a spoiled road postponed.

In spite of all the difficulties of traveling through *taryns* or detours and over the steep slopes covered with snow and underbrush, I remember with great pleasure the valley of the Dogdo River as the most picturesque part of the road between Verkhoyansk and Sredne-Koluimsk. The river passed through the Khas-Khaya-Ktakh Ridge and flowed in a deep wild valley with high stony slopes almost bare in some places and covered with fairly good forest in others. Under different circumstances, I would have spent several days there with a hammar in hand examining outcrops of rock, but now I could stop for barely half an hour, unless the lack of horses kept us longer. Unfortunately such delays always seemed to happen at stations far away from outcrops. Once, however, I did stop for a while at a small bare spot on the low shore composed of gravel, and was lucky enough to find a pebble with a few fossils. After examination and identification later in St. Petersburg, these fossils afforded me a chance to throw light on the geology of a wide area. How little is known of the geology of that part of Siberia! The fact that these fossils and my little discovery are still mentioned in descriptions of geology and geography of this part of the Yakutsk Province indicates that during the forty years which have passed since the time of our expedition, knowledge of the geology of the area has not advanced very far. The waste dimensions of the Province of Yakutsk equal seven times the area of prewar Germany, and the difficulty of access to its sub-Arctic and Arctic areas sufficiently excuse the apparent negligence of Russian scientists and explorers.

We left the Dogdo River and the system of the Yana and went over the high pass into the system of the Indigirka River. Our road was now for a while along the Selegnyak River, the left tributary of the Indigirka.

The divide between the Yana and Indigirka Rivers was the highest point of our route. We found here rather deep and abundant snow, which gave our horses hard work.

At the station on the Selegnyak River we found a few reindeer and could transport part of our baggage on sledges. We were still in saddles on the same horses which we rode from the Tostakh station. At the following station of Jabjaguin we found neither horses nor reindeer. I learned, however, that one reindeer owner, a Tungus, was still at his winter home a few miles away. I sent for him and persuaded him to give us reindeer to the next station, Kurelyakh. There were, however, only a few broken *nartas* at the station, which we immediately repaired. We also received several *nartas* from contractors whom we met there on their way back to Verkhoyansk. There was long discussion before they would give them to us, and I am sure that they finally dropped their objections only because they realized that I had decided to have the *nartas* with or without their consent.

Our delight in again driving reindeer was childlike. We could move twice as quickly as on horseback, and we could sit or lie on *nartas* and take a short nap without danger of falling. These were not the comfortable, covered *nartas* made for us at Yakutsk, but as long as spring weather prevailed it made no difference. The contractors told us that the ice on the Selegnyak River, which we would have to cross, was already weak. We broke through it once, but fortunately at a very shallow place.

At Kurelyak Station we met the returning messenger who had been sent to the Abyi Uprava from Verkhoyansk with the Ispravnik's order to prepare transportation for us. On the previous day he had broken through the ice on the Selegnyak River and having been soaked through had caught a bad cold. He told us that the authorities of the Uprava had begun eagerly to collect horses for us. When we again approached the Selegnyak River we met the postman going from Sredne-Koluimsk to Verkhoyansk. He also had had the bad luck to break through the ice. Although we could hardly expect to avoid a cold bath, we worried more about our instruments, particularly the chronometers, than about ourselves. The postman had marked with stocks the place where he had broken through the ice and had so located for us some comparatively shallow water, but we could scarcely expect that if our loaded sledges were to have the same misfortune, it would occur exactly at the marked place. The trouble was that, with the exception of the hole broken through by the postman, the river was still covered with ice. An open ford would have been better, for, the river being small, we could easily have selected shallow places for the crossing. River conditions reminded us that it was already the middle of May, although the road was still under snow. Temperatures in the middle of clear, sunny days were still below freezing. We met the post rather late in the afternoon and decided to wait until night. After sunset the temperature went down and by midnight dropped to five degrees.

The hole in the ice was still open and smoking in a very discomforting way. We decided to try crossing a few hundred feet from the road where the ice was intact. I took one end of a long leather strap, the other end of which was in the hands of our drivers, who were instructed to pull me out in case the ice should break. With careful steps I crossed the river safely, finding the ice stronger than I had hoped. We unharnessed the reindeer and with a long rope the drivers pulled the sledges over the ice. Then we let our reindeer go over two by two. In contrast to our predecessors we achieved a dry crossing, simply because we had left the beaten track.

Approaching the Abyi Uprava we were again dismayed by the lack of preparation for our travel in spite of the Verkhoyansk messenger's statements to the contrary. When on May seventeenth we arrived at the station of Abyi Uprava, I called immediately at the office of the uprava, a couple of miles from the station. Of the three or four people whom I met there, one particularly attracted my attention. He did not belong to the administration and I accepted him as a local trader. At the same time he was noticeably more intelligent than most of the traders. He used very correct Russian and spoke freely, without the slightest embarrassment, as a man who was accustomed to meet and speak with people of different rank. Later I learned that he was a self-defrocked Russian priest. Defrocked priests were very rare in Russia, as church authorities seldom applied that kind of punishment to their errant members. A self-defrocked priest was a still rarer phenomenon and perhaps this man was unique in all Russia. He defrocked himself in a very simple and impressive way. He called on the chief priest of his area and without any comment removed the large cross which every Russian priest wore on his breast, deposited it on the table before the surprised chief priest, and said: "Take it, I am not a priest any more."

In spite of this step, or perhaps because of it, among the natives he was greatly respected and was for them a person of great authority. My talk with him was interesting and enlightening. Our conversation concentrated upon the expedition and the troubles through which we were passing. He told me that, when a rumor of our coming had reached the natives, there had been some talk of a strike, and they had been ready to refuse to give us reindeer or horses. The strike would be directed not against us but against the Yakutsk administration, although we would be the sufferers. The reason for such a strike lay in the displeasure of the population with the mail contract. The regular post communication between Yakutsk and Sredne-Koluimsk had been organized rather recently. The contract between the administration and the people stated the approximate size of postal loads and, though actually the loads were much larger, the natives were obliged to carry the post for the price already fixed. After long talks, the Yakuts gave up the idea of a strike, perhaps because the order to supply our expedition with means of transportation was never sent from Yakutsk and they lacked an official command against which to strike.

Members of the uprava apologized because they were unable to make travel preparations for us, chiefly because of the season. The reindeer nomads had already moved to their summer pasturages and could not be found until the next autumn. For that reason it was impossible to replace the station reindeer completely exhausted after long and heavy winter work; condition of the roads prevented replacing reindeer by horses. The uprava's authorities assured me, however, that horses would be collected for my companions following me, and this was the most important thing to me.

As long as we traveled in the valley of the Selegnyak River we were among mountains connected with the system of the Khas-Khaya-Ktakh Ridge, gradually becoming lower toward the east. After we left the Selegnyak River, we took our way over endless plains, covered with rather poor, scarce, and exclusively larch forest. We crossed small elevations near the Indigirka River, and between this river and the Alazeya River. Although these elevations rose above the plains only a few hundred feet, they were bare on the top—clear proof that the forest was already fighting for its existence and could not stand even such a small change of altitude. Probably owing to their isolated position among the plains and also to their treeless tops, these small elevations became places of worship. On the tops of both hills I found piles of stones supporting sticks on which were suspended rags and horse hairs. In one place I found fifteen copeck coins laid between stones—a return to a paganism still firmly rooted among Yakuts, although officially all of them were sons of the Russian Orthodox Church. Until recently Yakuts have had *shamans*, or medicine men, who had great authority not only among natives but even among Russians.

On the plains we saw plenty of large and small lakes increasing in number with our movement toward the east. Clearances in the forest suggested swamps, and in summer the whole ground here would be soaked with water. Apparently such an abundance of surface water was in contradiction to the recognized dryness of the climate in northeastern Siberia, which compared with that of the Trans-Caspian region. In the latter area, however, a traveler found dry steppes and typical sand deserts. Cold climate explained fairly well this apparent contradiction. In northeastern Siberia precipitations were mostly in the form of snow, which evaporates more slowly than water. A small amount of snow not only was saved from evaporation but accumulated during the long winter. Permanently frozen ground did not permit rain and thaw water to penetrate deeply, and only a surface layer a few feet thick was soaked. Owing to a very level surface, outflow was not very active and was evident only during a short part of the year. In many places water was stagnant. Thus, three factors generally drying the ground—evaporation, ground water, and the surface outflow—were all very much retarded or even impossible in northeastern Siberia. The result was an area with a dry climate in a region of swamps and lakes.

On May eighteenth, we crossed the Indigirka River, which was still covered with rather strong ice. Spring, somewhat delayed for the last few days, came again. The road became worse and worse, but fortunately the route often lay over numerous lakes, and they were still covered with strong ice. The exhausted reindeer and the poor conditions of the road forced us to travel mostly at a foot pace, trotting a little only when going down hill. Unfortunately the next station, Baralin, was empty. The contractor, following the conditions of his contract,

had taken the reindeer from the station and in accordance
with local habits had not yet brought horses, although it
was almost two weeks after the sixth of May, when reindeer should have been replaced by horses. We waited for
the contractor for two days, not permitting the natives
from Abyi Uprava to start back, and then harnessed the
same reindeer and traveled with them about a hundred
and thirty miles more. The natives preferred to travel as
much as possible during the night when the roads were
frozen. Every twelve or fifteen miles we stopped to rest
our animals. In daytime the natives wanted to stop every
five miles or less to drink tea, and that always took at
least two or three hours. The tedium of such travel is
beyond description and a great part of this route I covered on foot. As the caravan never could overtake me, I
used my walking as a little ruse to prevent too many
stops. I waited for the caravan only when I estimated that
it was necessary to give the reindeer some rest, or when
I felt that a cup of tea would be welcome to me as well.

These days of enforced idleness, waiting for horses or
reindeer, and watching our natives who could leave us at
any time, were particularly nerve-wracking. We could
not do anything and had nothing to read. All conversation between us concerned the troubles through which
we passed and about the complete uncertainty of our expedition, the issue of which depended much on the
progress of our companions about whom we knew
nothing.

In this tortuous way we arrived at the Sygynlyak Station where we received a great and pleasant surprise in
comparatively good reindeer which we drove—not

dragged—over the road. From this station I sent ahead a messenger announcing our approach and we had no more delay until we reached our goal, Sredne-Koluimsk. We were now in the District of Koluimsk where for a long time everything had been in readiness for our coming. The local Ispravnik, as soon as he learned of our expedition, sent word to the population. As a result of his order, reindeer and horses were prepared for us. The only task of my messenger was to announce the very moment of our arrival. On May twenty-third a regular spring thawing began. Snow was soaked with water to such an extent that we wore slickers for protection against the splashes from reindeer hoofs.

At Yarmorskaya Station on the Alazeya River we said good-by to reindeer; the remaining hundred and twenty-five miles to Sredne-Koluimsk were covered on horseback. We expected the Alazeya River to be a menace. In some years this river, narrow at the place where it is crossed by the Sredne-Doluimsk Road, gets so much water in spring that the plain is flooded for a score of miles or more. There are no local accommodations for crossing such a body of water and I was told about travelers who waited more than a month for the falling of the spring water of the Alazeya River. We found only a small river lying deep between rather high shores and still covered with strong ice but, owing to the water on its surface, more slippery than I had chanced to observe anywhere. With extreme care we conveyed our baggage on sledges over the river. The station was just on the shore and it was unnecessary to take over horses.

Early in the morning of May twenty-seventh we arrived at Sredne-Koluimsk. Close to the town we were forced to make a detour on account of a small open river. We covered the distance from Yakutsk to Sredne-Koluimsk in thirty-seven days with an average speed of over forty miles per day. In the opinion of local people we were traveling very well, because under the same conditions people sometimes spent more than two months making the trip.

The Koluima River near the town was still covered with ice which, however, had already begun to move. The next day we saw a regular ice drive and my immediate departure from Sredne-Koluimsk to Nijne-Koluimsk was delayed, for in winter and summer the only way of communication between the towns was the river, by boats in summer, over the ice in winter.

8

THE LEPROSERY

SREDNE-KOLUIMSK is located on the left low shore of the Koluima River and we could see it from a distance of several miles. As in all Russian towns, the most conspicuous building was a church, a wooden structure dark from age, which some patriots of the town proudly called a cathedral. The contrast between the towering church and other buildings was greater than in other towns, for here the houses appeared to be pressed to the ground. As we approached the town, we realized that this effect was produced by the flat roofs of most of the houses. We saw flat roofs frequently in Siberia but at Sredne-Koluimsk they predominated. The flat roofs in the north of Yakutsk Province are also good proof of the dry climate and meager amount of precipitation. I saw the town in February; snow had been accumulating for about six months but the roofs were by no means over-loaded. Nor were there any rains to soak the few inches of earth on the roof in summer.

The capital of a wide territory, the town nevertheless was made to appear rather depressive by all these block houses darkened by time and untouched by paint. The vista did not become better when we walked through the wide irregular streets—squares rather than streets—which were used only by pedestrians; the streets of Sredne-Koluimsk appeared strangely empty compared with other provincial Russian towns. After a while we realized that the absence of small domestic animals was responsible for such emptiness. The most important northern domesticated animal, the dog, would not stand alienation of affection by sheep, pigs, cats, and chickens, and would dispose of them quickly if they were introduced.

My first concern at Sredne-Koluimsk was to eliminate as many difficulties as possible from Kozhevnicov's and Weber's travel along the road over which I had just passed. I had no idea where they were and could not direct my assistance to any definite point. At my request, the Ispravnik of the Koluima District sent six horses at once to the first station west of Sredne-Koluimsk. Reinforced in this way, that station had to send six horses further west to the next station. The latter had to repeat the same for the following station, and so on. Somewhere between Sredne-Koluimsk and Verkhoyansk six horses should meet our caravan. I recognized that the Koluima administration showed a great zeal, if not always a corresponding skill, in assisting our expedition. Unfortunately we could not utilize this zeal at the proper time, on account of the red tape through which I had passed in St. Petersburg. As I have mentioned, Governor Kraft's telegram was received at Sredne-Koluimsk on the second of April. About two weeks before that day, the Lamut contractors were at Sredne-Koluimsk with a great number of first-grade reindeer. It would have been easy to purchase from them all animals necessary for the expedition, had St. Petersburg's officials permitted Governor Kraft and me to issue necessary orders before the money for the expedition formally was assigned.

By the time Governor Kraft's telegram arrived, the Sredne-Koluimsk administration could not collect as many reindeer as we needed, and those they supplied, apparently from the station stock, were gaunt and exhausted from their long winter work. The telegram arrived also after the Chukchi Fair held every year at Panteleikha Village. I expected that during this fair, visited by the natives of the northeastern part of Arctic Siberia, the Chukchi would at least learn of the expedition. Certainly here was a good opportunity to introduce us as government officials and to repeal the announcement about approaching Turukhansk exiles. The opportunity, however, was missed.

To my satisfaction I learned that all supplies ordered from St. Petersburg had been found at Sredne-Koluimsk and forwarded to the embouchure of the Chaun River where a depot was stocked with provisions. With some uneasiness I realized that Sredne-Koluimsk had been on short rations of butter and sugar on account of filling our orders.

Among other orders our telegram gave advice for the method of handling supplies which could be spoiled by moisture. For dried bread, special boxes were covered on the outside with sheet iron and soldered along the seams. Unfortunately the dimensions of the boxes were made according to the size of the iron sheets. As a result, one of the boxes weighed five hundred and twenty-four pounds, and several people were needed to load it on a sledge. Later I was not surprised to find the same box at Nijni-Koluimsk, for nobody would carry such a heavy, unwieldy load hundreds of miles to the Chaun River over a none too smooth road with *nartas* not constructed for the transportation of this kind of shipment.

The small town was quite excited over our arrival. Everyone wanted to see us and converse with us. We found it interesting to meet the local people and to get different information for our future work, or to hear about parts of the country which we would be unable to visit. Everywhere our calls were carried on in the same way, whatever the time of day. Hardly had we time to take seats when tea was served. We realized that almost every hostess had her samovar "under steam" all the time. Before we were through with tea a *zacusca* was served. A *zacusca* might be compared with the American appetizer, but the *zacusca* in Russia, and particularly in Siberia, is a meal by itself. Syedov, who knew little about hospitality in Sredne-Koluimsk, was almost dead after our first day's visits. The town reminded us in some way of Yakutsk during the Easter holiday, only here the holiday was a climatic, or seasonal, one. The long winter was over. Days were warm but not hot, and already very long. Mosquitoes, which in northern Siberia spoil summertime completely, had not yet come. The people had just received their supplies from Yakutsk and could enjoy many palatable things of which they would soon be short or lack altogether. They were having a sort of vacation because every business except home business had stopped. No natives coming for trade, no trade travels to natives!

The fishing season had not yet begun and, besides that, fishing was the main occupation of only a few people in Sredne-Koluimsk.

Sometimes there were evening parties, usually with cards. Games were played with comparatively large sums of money. I saw people gambling with hundreds of rubles, who, judging from their appearance, could scarcely own a part of this sum. They were playing very quietly, gaining without showing any joy and losing without apparent grief, completely self-controlled. Syedov tried his luck one evening and the next day was very angry with himself. Many among the local people had more money than one might think from the appearances of their houses, clothing, and general way of living. They had, however, no good ways to spend it. They were much interested in our instruments and in their prices. When Syedov told them that the value of a chronometer was 450 rubles, they were surprised, but later some of them were considering the possibility of buying such an expensive watch. They liked good, dependable things but could not find them, even at Yakutsk. A high price was for them a sign of good value, especially if they learned the price from such a traveler as Syedov, who did not sell his equipment and, if he did, would do so without cheating.

At one party I met a Red Cross nurse who was in charge of a leprosery close to the town. Leprosy was a rather common sickness in Yakutsk Province, but besides this small leprosery near Sredne-Koluimsk there was only one more in the District of Viluisk, the latter of much larger size and better equipped. The official director of the leprosery was a local doctor who had been in the Koluima District for two years. Since dealing with lepers was considered a dangerous job, the doctor and nurse enjoyed special pension privileges. One year of service counted for three and a half years, and while other Russian medical men received their pensions after thirty-five years, at Sredne-Koluimsk full pension was earned after ten years of service. Besides the leprosery, the doctor also had in his care a territory of about a thousand miles in diameter, being the only doctor in this whole immense area. No wonder that the medicine men had such a strong hold on the population! I was told that the doctor never visited the leprosery, but put all the work on the shoulders of his nurse. Nevertheless he was to receive all pension rights. Local society and administration did not protest such negligence, since they would have been afraid of the doctor had he actually come in contact with lepers. I noticed at once that they were afraid of the nurse.

Next day the nurse expected to visit her lepers and invited me to go along. The leprosery was located on the other side of the river a few miles up from the town and about a mile from the shore. Living quarters were the regular *yurtas* of the Yakuts, with their open fireplaces. In Southern Siberia and Turkestan a *yurta* is a felt tent used by nomads. In the province of Yakutsk this name was also applied to wooden houses of a very primitive construction.

In the first stage of the disease the skins of lepers lose their sensitivity. Insensible to pain, the patients often would burn their hands to blisters while warming them before the open fire. The first lepers who met us had such blisters on their arms, although apparently otherwise they were very little affected by the terrible malady. Altogether there were about a score of people at the leprosery. Two of them were in very poor condition, and I learned later that they died shortly after our visit. It was chiefly for their benefit that the nurse visited the place when I accompanied her. She had brought the two patients new shirts and trousers made of cheap cotton stuff to be put on after their death. I never shall forget how one of them tried to raise his head to look at the new trousers and how, still groaning, he tried to say something to express his gratitude for them.

The leprosery left upon me a very painful impression. It was poor, dirty, and did not remind one of a hospital at all. However, it was much better for lepers to live thus in a sort of colony than to dwell in isolated *yurtas* on the forested shore of some lake, far away from any settlement, as was customary among Yakuts. Such a hermit would be visited from time to time by someone who would leave food on the ground and run away when the leper appeared. If the leper was not seen for some time a careful investigation would be made and it would be found that he had died. A quick burial followed; the *yurta* and all the belongings of the leper would be burned, and a sigh of relief would be breathed by the local community!

In such a leprosery as the one I visited, the lepers were bound together by a sense of mutual sympathy. Those who were stronger helped the weaker or dying. During our visit the men who met us reported immediately the general conditions of the colony. The nurse visited them often, listening to their lamentations, dressing their wounds, giving such medical help as was necessary, and, last but not least, bringing to dying men new shirts and trousers. Never in my life have I been more impressed by the comfort the dying find in little rites. In our society when a dying individual gives instructions about how his or her body is to be dressed we are apt to call it sentimentality and to make fun of it. Yet here was a savage showing the same feelings, craving a small attention— new trousers by which he thought his dying would be made easier.

Shortly after my visit to the leprosery I went to see the Ispravnik. He looked at me with ill-concealed terror. Probably if I had not been a traveler from St. Petersburg, *persona grata*, he would have requested me not to visit him immediately after having been at the leprosery.

While we enjoyed the local hospitality and became friends with many people we were at the same time disagreeably surprised by the greed of people who wanted to sell us something for the expedition. By no means could their prices be called friendly. When we were buying something (I do not speak about buying merchandise of more or less fixed value) or hiring workmen, there was always a long bargaining, and business was always represented as some kind of sacrifice for our benefit. If a man sold us something, it was always with an expression of regret, although he had received a double or triple price. The long bargaining probably is the result of habit with natives to whom the procedure of trade is not less important and agreeable than the end of it.

Exaggerated prices apparently were based on an idea that expeditions like ours were unlimited in their financial means.

We wanted several boats—Syedov for his work, I for transportation of the expedition. There were plenty of boats on the shore which could not be used without repairs, but nobody wished to sell us one or two. After several days of unsuccessful attempts to buy them, we told the Ispravnik that we would have to make a requisition and pay for the boats according to the estimation of administration and several private individuals. Immediately boats were offered for sale in even greater number than we needed. I bought one which was in very poor shape and hired an idle workman to repair it, paying him fifteen rubles and a bottle of vodka for about a day of half-hearted activity. When we launched the boat and began to load, she at once filled with water. The workman explained that he considered himself obliged only to patch a big hole on the bottom of the boat, not to make any general repairs.

Syedov needed a much better boat than I, one in which he could sail on the sea. As soon as he bought a boat and hired for his crew three young and rather clever Cossacks, he began immediately to adapt her for his purpose. He belonged to the class of mariners who had studied the sea and sea craft from boyhood. His task was not easy, for the Koluima boats were typical of those found on all Siberian rivers, boats with wide flat bottoms, low boards, and rather high-pointed bows and sterns which were similar in shape. The boats which we saw on the Koluima River were of very poor construction, with oars that suggested shovels. Syedov raised the boards, made new oars, and put up a mast which, supplied with a small sail, became a great sensation in the town. He had, however, no means of making a centerboard and never could navigate his boat satisfactorily.

The observatory at Irkutsk asked me to organize at Sredne-Koluimsk a meteorological station. I had brought along the parts of a mercurial barometer and the necessary amount of mercury. In spite of the fact that Sredne-Koluimsk is larger than Verkhoyansk and had several people who, in my opinion, had leisure enough to carry on observations, I could not find an observer, although the Observatory was ready to pay a small salary. Some people were ready to do such work, but only for immediate remuneration, which the Observatory could not pay. The amount asked by them for this supplementary work was pretty near the salaries which those people had been paid by the government for a regular job as a teacher or a clerk. I fixed the barometer and left the other instruments at the home of the local priest in the hope that his wife would be glad to have her own if small earning, but the hope did not materialize.

All through the end of May the weather was mostly cloudy, but in June it cleared, and on the fourth we made combined astronomical observation at Sredne-Koluimsk.

Time passed. The river was probably ice-free to its embouchure. Summer had begun, when the "sun does not sleep." Trees showed leaves. In the middle of the day mosquitoes increased their activity. We did not hear anything about our companions, and local people did not expect them soon. Rivers, lakes, and swamps could now sometimes prove an almost impassable hindrance. Syedov, the reconstruction of his ship completed, could begin his work in the embouchure of the Koluima River and was ready to leave for Nijne-Koluimsk. I had no more business in Sredne-Koluimsk either and decided to leave with Syedov.

9

TCHERSKI'S GRAVE

WE LEFT Sredne-Koluimsk June the seventh. Syedov, traveling with his own crew to do all the work, soon left me behind, for I had to change rowers at every station, although I had my own boat. I was in no great hurry, for I still hoped to see the rest of the party. I was anxious also to investigate the geology of the valley, particularly of the right shore of the river, since everywhere the left shore of the Koluima River is of alluvial origin. In local terminology, the right shore of the Koluima is called the "Kamenny," or rocky shore, while the left one is known as the "Zemlyano," or earth shore. The left shore has a uniform and low height, whereas the right shore attains in places a great altitude, and protrudes into the river in the form of high, picturesque capes separated from each other by alluvial planes and corresponding to the embouchures of smaller and larger tributaries. I found, on the right shore, marine limestones with fossils which at that time I considered as Devonian, sandstones in which I thought it would be possible to discover coal, and plenty of eruptive rocks such as basalts or diabases, and different porphyries. The right shore of the Koluima is nothing else than a border of the high land located east of this river and spreading northward to the Arctic Ocean. The work on the Koluima had thus a close connection with the work of the expedition on the Arctic Coast.

The Cossack whom I took from Sredne-Koluimsk was very busy all the first day bailing water from our leaking boat which we could not completely repair until the first stop for the night. I could have traveled all twenty-four hours, but I did not want to miss anything worth seeing. For several days we enjoyed fine calm weather and had a very pleasant journey. The great river was rather deserted, as the summer fishing had not yet begun, but here and there we met small groups of fishermen. Once we came across a fellow traveling in a *vyetka*, a one-man boat with bottom and sides made of three thin boards. A very light boat, it had good speed, but was extremely unstable on water and required great skill in handling. I knew how to handle one of these light boats but I decided to act the fool. I told the owner that I wished to try a *vyetka*, inquired how to sit in it, how to row with double paddle, and so on. Two people steadied the *vyetka* at both ends as I sat down as clumsily as I could without upsetting it. Paddle in hands, I ordered them to let me alone. As I cranked the *vyetka* this way and that, almost upsetting her, my workmen jumped into our boat and tried to follow me as closely as possible. But very soon I left them behind, and after making a tour of the river brought the *vyetka* back to her owner who, with my crew, admired me for learning so quickly. Many months later the Ispravnik at Sredne-Koluimsk told me this story in a much exaggerated form. In his version there was stormy weather and big waves on the river which I had crossed safely in a *vyetka* when nobody else dared to leave the shore. That is one of the ways by which heroes are very often made!

On June eleventh we met a rather strong north wind. In my attempt to sail around the Khanjibay Cape, I almost wrecked my boat, and I was forced to stop for the night before reaching the station. At our forced night camp we met the Chief of Police of the Nijne-Koluimsk area, the so-called *Zasyedatel*, Melnicov by name. He had left for Sredne-Koluimsk to find out what had happened to the expedition. After our meeting he turned back to Nijne-Koluimsk to give me his help there. In some ways the *Zasyedatel*, about whom I was told in St. Petersburg, was a remarkable person. He had been sent to the Koluima District as a young political exile during the last decade of the past century. He belonged to the group of political exiles from which were developed later several noted scientists whose exploration and research concerning the local native tribes was supported by the Russian Geographical Society and its Siberian branches. Melnicov was not engaged in such scientific research, but his career was rather unusual for a political exile, and so successful that at the time of our expedition he was second only to the Ispravnik or Chief of the whole Koluimsk District.

Nevertheless, he was still an exile and never free to leave northeastern Siberia and visit his former home. New generations of political exiles sent to the Koluima District in the beginning of this century returned home in the autumn of 1905 in triumph and were greeted as heroes by the local people, but ex-exile Melnicov was still an exile in fact. In 1909 there were no other political exiles at Sredne-Koluimsk or Nijne-Koluimsk either, except Melnicov. I do not think he felt at that time much more independent than when he had been an exile by law. He still had a boss, the *Ispravnik* of the Koluima District, who could dismiss him at any time. He was already closely bound to the place of his exile; he had a family, some property, and was intimately engaged in the interests of the local life. From a few words of Governor Kraft's I understood that Melnicov had been one of the local men who could have carried on such exploration as was entrusted to me. Melnicov was ordered to make all necessary preparations for the expedition and travel with us if I required it. In his work for us he showed great zeal, but neither skill nor the ability to deal with local people and conditions. In the two days he was with the expedition, he was more harmful than useful, although quite unintentionally. The expedition was for him only an opportunity to climb up in his position. He was very eager to be decorated for his work and even asked me directly about it.

During the Russian Revolution I used to ponder over Melnicov's fate. I never heard about him and did not know if he managed to save his head. All members of the police were in a dangerous position at that time and a man with such a record as Melnicov's could scarcely escape great danger. To his credit it is necessary to say that he never used his former connections in the interests of his new job. His former friends, ex-exiles, were quite positive in this matter. The revolutionary mob would neither know nor believe such a sense of honor in a policeman, but every member of the mob would remember that Melnicov had been a political exile and, by becoming a member of the local administration, had betrayed the work of the revolutionists.

Because of the strong opposite wind and rough water we moved very slowly from the Khanjibay Cape and proceeded only to a place which brought to my memory another political exile whose fate was, however, entirely different from that of Melnicov. On the shore of a new channel washed through by the river we found a modest cross with the inscription, "At this place died on June 25, 1892, Tcherski, the leader of the expedition of the Imperial Academy of Sciences." A young man, Tcherski was exiled to Siberia for participation in the Polish uprising. He had only an elementary education, but at Irkutsk he met a group of educated Poles, also exiles, naturalists of different specialities, who had already started on an exploration of the new and unknown country. Some of them later became internationally known. The last of this group, the zoologist Dybovski, former professor of Cracow University, died only a few years ago, well in his nineties. These young scientists were supported by the Siberian Branch of the Russian Geographical Society in Irkutsk. They had not only a place to report and discuss their work but a fairly good library, a museum in which to deposit their materials, and magazines in which to publish their papers. Tcherski joined this group and began to work on Post-Tertiary fossil animals which were well represented at the Irkutsk Museum and in general were very common in Siberia. Very soon Tcherski became an expert in that field. He worked also on the geology of Siberia, touching the most difficult and important problems, and achieved a great success in this field as well. He published much, acquired considerable popularity, and through his service for science gained his freedom.

He moved to St. Petersburg and was working there at the Zoological Museum of the Russian Academy of Sciences. In 1891 the Academy commissioned him to go for three years into the northeastern part of Siberia for geological and, particularly, paleontological investigations in his field of Post-Tertiary mammals. It was a sort of free exile into which Tcherski took his wife and their son, a boy over ten years old. Unfortunately, Tcherski's health was already broken; he had tuberculosis and this last enterprise was for his friends a source of very deep concern. Tcherski passed the winter at Verkhne-Koluimsk and apparently felt well. In the spring, however, his sickness took a bad turn. He arrived by boat at Sredne-Koluimsk as an invalid and left it almost dying. He traveled, dying in his boat, all the time observing the geology of the shore with the assistance of his wife and boy; following his instructions, they examined outcrops, obtained specimens, and wrote notes. The diary of this period was mostly written by the boy. A few days of travel passed as Tcherski became weaker and weaker. Near the place where we found the cross the expedition had landed. To everyone and to Tcherski himself it was clear that this was the end. With a weak voice, Tcherski gave his wife and son his last instructions; he told them how to liquidate the expedition and what to do with the collections, instruments, and other supplies. Blood out of his throat was suffocating him and stopping his speech. His wife helped him remove the coagulated blood from his mouth with forceps. The widow buried the body on the Omalon station located in the front of the embouchure of the Omalon River, made a fence around the grave, put a cross upon it, and fixed it as well as she could. We found the place in very poor shape.

Many years after Tcherski's death, his son, then a university student, worked at the Geological Museum of the Academy of Science which was in my care. Collections of their expedition were at our museum and I let the boy work with them. He found diaries written by his own hand, specimens collected by him and his mother, and apparently recollected every moment of that sad happening although he was then only a boy. I remembered very well what he had told me when, during my expedition, I visited the places of his father's death and burial.

Somewhere near the embouchure of the Omalon River on the right shore of the Koluima River was fixed the primary location of Nijne-Koluimsk, but the site was changed because of the fate of the first workmen. A party of about a dozen men had begun construction of houses. One day a workman left his party for a while. When he returned a few hours later, he found his companions dead or dying around a kettle of fish soup. He gave the remnants of the soup to his dog, which died shortly in convulsions. He remembered that in the morning catch of fish had been a one-eyed sturgeon and now he realized that it was the fish that poisoned the soup. This accident scared the authorities so much that the selected and rather convenient place was abandoned, and Nijne-Koluimsk was built up where it is now, on the low left shore of the river.

We arrived at Nijne-Koluimsk very early in the morning of June fifteenth and found Syedov still in the town, making his last preparations. Nijne-Koluimsk hardly has the right to be called a town, still less a fortress, which name recently was applied to it officially. Even for a village it was a miserable settlement. It had a very old church with one or two mica windows, but it had no permanent priest. The town was almost empty, or at least it looked empty when I arrived. Taking my morning ablution, I was not afraid I would embarrass anybody when I jumped out to the street in the nude to throw out the water.

The best but still a poor house had been prepared for the expedition and I lived there several days. The first thing I found were large boxes of dried bread, which had been delivered with great difficulty here and no farther. If these boxes were to reach their destination, the Chaun depot, it was necessary to transport them in more convenient form. Rock specimens collected on the river needed boxes as well. I asked Melnicov to find a carpenter to build the new boxes. When the fellow came I explained what I wanted and asked the price. Without hesitation he named a figure at least ten times higher than that kind of work should cost. When I told him that it was beyond any reasonable limit, he said, "Maybe, but it is now the fishing time." I asked him if they were fishing already. "Not yet," he answered quietly enough. I sent him away and made the boxes myself. Fortunately, or perhaps unfortunately, I had time for such work.

Speaking with the carpenter, I was surprised that I had to make an effort to understand him, for, although he was Russian and spoke his native tongue, it was the Lower Koluimsk dialect. I could not relate the origin of this dialect with the Chukchi language spoken here by almost everyone, nor with any other native language. It was an original corruption of language similar to what children do with their mother tongue. Some Russian words were so mispronounced that I could hardly recognize them. I was, for example, quite sure that the name of Kanjebai Cape on the Koluima River was of native origin, but when I tried to find out its meaning, I realized that the name was Russian and very appropriately applied. At the same time, in the folklore of the Lower Koluima people one discovers a great many old Russian songs which have been preserved there through centuries while they have been forgotten in the European Russian from which they had come to the Koluima River. A few of the songs dealt with matters absolutely strange to the place. I wrote down a song in which repeated reference was made to a grape. Very few people on the Lower Koluima, if any, had the slightest idea what a grape was!

I was confronted now with the final organization of the expedition, and before all else I had to find the whereabouts of the reindeer which had been brought for the expedition and pastured somewhere in the area of lower

Koluima in the care of a hired Lamut. From the reports handed to me at Sredne-Koluimsk I knew that the expedition would have not nearly the number of reindeer ordered from St. Petersburg and that the quality of the herd would be low. At that season it was not possible to find any more reindeer, but since in summer horses could be used as well, I decided to add horses to the outfit.

I sent one messenger for a local trader by the name of Soloveiv who, I was told, had many horses. Another messenger had to bring the head of the local community, Shculev, and the third was sent after the chief of the local Cossacks. All those people lived far away and were remote from one another. Thus it was necessary to spend several days waiting. On the eighteenth of June, Soloviev arrived and sold me twelve horses, six of which had to be broken in. At Nijne-Koluimsk I found one more horse, and Shculev, who had arrived on June twentieth, sold us two more. Thus I was able to buy fifteen horses but no more, and I was not going to be able to make all the travel exclusively with horses. There was also an insufficiency of saddles, pads, and girths, and it was necessary to look for them everywhere or to make new ones.

In the meantime the news about our reindeer was disheartening. For a while they had been pastured on the right side of the Koluima River, but shortly before the breaking of the ice, Lamut shepherds tending our herd had crossed the river and moved into the tundras of the left shore, and it was here that a search for them must be made. On the right side of the river only twenty-nine reindeer were collected from a number of owners. I immediately commissioned Melnicov to find reindeer on the left side of the Koluima River and bring them over to our side.

June seventeenth brought fine, sunny weather and we could again make simultaneous astronomical observations, I with my own universal instrument but with Syedov's chronometers, and he with his sextant. Unfortunately, not having along the Nautical Almanac, we missed the moment of the sun's eclipse, which happened that day. The next day Syedov left for the lower Koluima to begin his work there. I could not leave until two days later.

I had no hope of my companions' overtaking me during the summer and decided to go along. I had enough reindeer and horses, instruments and arms. Syedov planned to determine as soon as possible several basic astronomical points and then give me two chronometers from the four which he carried.

On June twenty-first at three o'clock in the morning, quite unexpectedly Kozhevnicov arrived. He was rawboned and looked somewhat older than before. Our reunion was marked by a sense of victory. We still had about three months of warmth and almost continuous daylight, so we anticipated doing something besides struggling against conditions where success counted neither for the expedition nor for our own glory. Weber was behind because he had stopped at one station on the river to observe the solar eclipse which Syedov and I had missed. Jucov, poor fellow, they had left at Kyurelyakh Station in the Verkhoyansk District west of the Indigirea and Alazeya Rivers which were always a serious menace at this time of the year. Neither of these rivers, however, proved serious hindrances for my companions. Apart from such conditions as the lack of horses and the large caravan, the main reason for their delay was the well-progressed spring. They had not had the benefit of the use of reindeer, which from time to time had helped us so much. They were also forced to use the longer summer road, making a great number of detours around lakes.

I could spend only a few hours with Kozhevnicov, and at ten o'clock left Nijne-Koluimsk to push the preparations for the next lap of travel. Kozhevnicov hardly had time to tell me in a general way about his journey with the caravan. As a matter of fact, I never did get from him any detailed report. For the rest of the time we were too busy with everyday happenings. I avoided asking him too many questions, for I could judge from his conduct that the past experience was mostly very painful. His nerves were in bad shape. I thought sometimes that had I been in his position I should have managed the work differently, but I could not criticize him too much for I did not know all the difficulties that had confronted him. I hoped to get from him a written report to add to the records of our expedition, but it never materialized, owing partly to the adverse conditions of the post-expeditionary time.

10

LAPTEV'S TOWER

LEAVING Nijne-Koluimsk, we had good proof of the sparsity of population in northeastern Siberia, even along the rivers where to a great extent settlements were concentrated. Travels of members of the expedition and our messengers almost exhausted the stock of free labor at Nijne-Koluimsk. For my boat I could hire only two rowers and I, myself, had to do the steering.

On the night of June twenty-first I landed at a small settlement on the Panteleikha Creek, and for three days stayed at Soloviev's. This settlement was the site of the early spring fair visited by the Chukchi. The place had certainly some importance since Soloviev, one of the most enterprising men in the district, had settled there. Three generations had lived under the roof of Soloviev's house, and this fact gave me a chance to make a very interesting observation. Eighteenth-century travelers in Siberia mentioned more than once the wide occurrence of syphilis. The traveler Gmelin wrote about his doubts in using privies and mentioned observing many people with defective noses. For my part, I had heard not infrequent allusions to some suspicious illnesses three or four generations back which in all probability were of syphilitic nature. Stories of this kind were often told by direct descendants of possible syphilitics who did not think that they might be afflicted with the terrible disease of their grandparents. Northeastern Siberia, particularly the Koluima District, had a very bad reputation in this respect.

Travelers of our generation had no such impressions as that of their predecessors. During travels in different parts of Siberia I met people with disfigured faces, but hardly in greater number than anywhere else. At the same time I knew very well that medical help, even in the southern part of Siberia, never was adequate and was absolutely lacking in many northern areas. The healing of syphilis requires long and systematic treatment which only a few patients can afford even in areas where there are doctors, hospitals, and necessary drugs. In time one comes to the conclusion that syphilis disappears perhaps by taking on a milder form in each succeeding generation. Soloviev's family showed very distinctly such a passing away of the disease. His father, an old man in his seventies, had a caved-in nose. Soloviev himself, with whom I contracted business, was a strong, well-built man of middle age with a good color of skin, full of health and energy. He had about ten boys and girls, all healthy, good-looking people whom no one would suspect of having a syphilitic grandfather.

Soloviev, his family and workman, and my boatmen worked very hard all the time. I was lucky enough to find saddles and saddletrees, but it was necessary to make pads of sacks filled with hay and sewed through in different directions with strong thread. A number of new girths were made of horse hair, with buckles partly hammered on the spot. Then began the breaking in of those horses which had never before been used. I feel deeply obliged to Soloviev that in a very short time he managed to train quite wild horses so that we could use them. That partly excused his exhorbitant prices.

Meanwhile, I prepared all the baggage from Nijne-Koluimsk for transportation on horseback. I then made a geological excursion to the hill near the settlement. Soloviev also sold me a *cayuk*, a small boat made from one tree and somewhat similar to the American canoe, which we used frequently. In response to my telegram from St. Petersburg ordering two small boats, three *vyetkas* were bought for us, one of them already sent to the Chaum Depot, and two at Nijne-Koluimsk. I realized immediately that they were chosen with no consideration of the character of our future work; Soloviev's *cayuk* was exactly what we wanted.

Early in the morning of June twenty-seventh our party at last united at the settlement of Sukharnoye on the eastern shore of the embouchure of the Koluima River. At this point we should have brought together all our means of transportation and started on the expedition. A whole week had passed since I had sent Zasyedatel Melnicov to look for our reindeer on the western side of the Koluima River. From Sukharnoye, I sent our new interpreter, Yucaguir Rumyanzev, to the east, where, according to our information, were pastured on the Medvyzhya River, along with reindeer belonging to Soloviev, twenty animals bought for the expedition.

Soloviev permitted us to take from his herd thirty animals more, certainly for a high price. We had acquired, however, a habit of not being surprised at the appetite of local people for the pocketbook of the expedition. Two days later Rumyanzev came back without reindeer. Soloviev's shepherd and the whole herd had moved in an unknown direction. On the same day that Rumyanzev arrived at Sukharnoye, Melnicov succeeded in bringing seventy-one reindeer over the Koluima River. The reindeer were brought over at a village having the rather picturesque name of Krai Lyesov, which meant "limit of forests." North of this settlement the Koluima River flows through tundras. One animal was drowned and fifty-three could not be driven into water at all, but remained on the western shore of the river and were thus lost to us. Lamut shepherds refused to go back to the right shore of the river and only with great reluctance did they obey Melnicov when he ordered them to return. He brought along in his boat some harness and several sledges of the Chukchi construction, although I had very explicitly ordered from St. Petersburg sledges of the kind used by Lamuts, which would be much better for our work.

Winter and summer alike, the Arctic tundras do not know any other carriage but the sledge. The reason is the absence of any summer road on which a wheeled carriage could move, with the exception of the elevations where it is possible to find graveled places fairly smooth for a few miles. Mostly it is necessary to go through endless swamps full of bumps and holes where wheels and axles would be quickly broken, and even on elevations, when the tundras become dry, the bumps and holes remain. A sledge glides over a wet grassy tundra fairly well, although certainly not so well as on snow. I have traveled by sledge over shore gravel, but it required not less than four good reindeer, fresh every day, and new runners almost as often. With few exceptions (the chronometer box and instruments) our baggage could be carried on reindeer back. I had expected to use reindeer chiefly during spring traveling over snow and from St. Petersburg had ordered only sledges. According to my calculations I had plenty of time to prepare everything necessary for traveling in summer fashion while moving two or three months with reindeer breeders. Now everything was different. It was absolutely impossible to find the number of pack saddles or saddletrees, straps, and other equipment needed by our party, and just as impossible to construct all those paraphernalia, particularly with the help of natives whom I very soon knew to be poor, lazy people with no initiative or stamina.

Two more days passed before our reindeer herd arrived at Sukharnoye. I was never prepared for such poor animals for which we paid prices much higher than average. I could compare them only with those reindeer which we had used during our travel to Sredne-Koluimsk, animals exhausted after a whole winter of strenuous work. These animals had been pastured for about a month on fresh grass. Pressure behind their ears failed to reveal even one deer with a small lump of fat. I had expected to have fresh animals, but, judged from the show of their rib, the reindeer had been worked hard during the past winter, and had not been given any rest by the Lamuts who had been using them all the spring. Fourteen reindeer were old, almost toothless, quite unable to gain weight under the most favorable conditions. For their long working life they deserved a complete rest, not participation in an expedition. With great difficulty our Lamuts covered forty miles in two days, although the reindeer were not heavily loaded.

The Lamuts who arrived with the herd as our drivers and shepherds were reindeerless paupers instead of the owners of good herds of reindeer whom I had expected to have at my service. Lamuts owned altogether only eight animals, but with their belongings they required thirty for transport purposes. Expecting to travel with reindeer breeders, I was quite sure that I should always have a good supply of fresh meat, and certainly had no thought that it would be necessary to feed them. The first appeal to me from our Lamuts was for bread and meat. Fortunately I had ordered plenty of dried bread and was able to meet this request. I saw that the number of Lamuts was too large and felt that it was very important to rid ourselves of some of them, but I could not do it right now as I wished to be a little better acquainted with the people. I decided to move the crowd a few miles north to Laptev's Signal Tower and there reorganize the whole personnel of the expedition. The advance guard, Weber and the Cossack Domashonkin, had moved on the day before. From a tower we planned to begin our survey of the coast, and Weber had to make there an astronomical observation.

Dmitry Laptev, a member of the Russian Great

Northern Expedition who described in 1741 the part of the Siberian Arctic shore east of the Koluima River, built the signal tower known by his name. In spite of age, the tower, as well as the small adjacent barracks, was still in fairly good condition. The tower, about twenty-five to thirty feet high, was in the form of a pyramid cut off on the top by a flat platform. It was located on the high shore and could be seen from the sea and river. Its construction showed well that even at that time, almost two hundred years ago, naval people had thought about the possibility of navigation on the Koluima and had tried to mark the entrance into the river. The platform on the top of the tower probably was a place to put a signal fire or flag. These dreams of navigation on the Koluima materialized only after our expedition in 1911, when for the first time a steamer arrived at Nijne-Koluimsk from Vladivostok, exactly a hundred and seventy years after Laptev's work. The signal tower had waited a long time for discovery by an approaching ship. I do not know if the tower still exists; it is not mentioned in the last Russian Pilot available to me, or in the Arctic Pilot of the English Admiralty.

At last, on the fourth of July, our horses arrived. Still wild, the horses in passing through the forests had damaged loads and harness and injured themselves. The grooms were completely tired out. They had been hired along the route—one was taken by Melnicov almost by force from the shore of the river where he was fishing at that time. Shculev, from whom I bought two horses and who joined the expedition, had helped with his own workmen. At Sukharnoye, one more groom was hired.

All the day of July fourth was used for distribution of the baggage into separate loads, packing and weighing. The last operation was very important, for the side loads of one pack had to be as nearly equal in weight as possible. When the loads were ready, grooms bound them with leather straps in such a way that every load had a loop on the top which could be connected with the corresponding loop of the other side. More time was spent in the mending of harnesses. The next day, July fifth, we began to make final preparations for moving to Laptev's Tower. At the tower we had yet more baggage, brought over by Weber in the boat. Fortunately it was chiefly Aesop's load, provisions which would diminish every day. During these preparations we noticed on the river a sail approaching the village: it was Jucov, whom we did not expect to see at all. He brought along three horse-loads of brick tea and tobacco, substitutes for money in the area of our future travel.

When grooms approached the wild horses with saddles, they grew quite mad and began to kick and bite and try to run away. All the population of Sukharnoye turned out to give us a helping hand, but they did more harm than good with their noise and their incessant jostling and dashing about this way and another. I remember how one horse tore loose, reared, and, not finding any place to run, tried to jump on the flat roof of a small warehouse. The spectacle gave much amusement to the inhabitants of Sukharnoye; they stood around voicing unprintable remarks for the benefit of the grooms who were in no mood for banter.

Shortly after noon everything was ready and about

two o'clock I, with Kizhevnicov, left for Laptev's Tower where we arrived that evening. Later the horse caravan arrived. They had made a fairly long detour around the small rivers which could not be forded. The reindeer caravan arrived at two o'clock the next morning. Rumyanzev, who was traveling with this caravan, confirmed my conviction that the reindeer were a very bad lot. They could hardly pull even a light load, and frequently dropped on all fours, always a sign of extreme fatigue. From time to time it was necessary to change harnessed animals for fresh ones and give them time out for rest.

At Laptev's Tower I revised all my Lamut staff. Altogether I had three families. The leader of the Lamuts, Alexey, had along two daughters and at the next camp we expected to have his two sons and their friend. Alexey I held responsible for the fate of the reindeer in crossing the Koluima River. This blunder had cost us over a week of time and fifty-three reindeer which could not be brought back, plus one drowned. I could not trust Alexey any more and did not like to have him in the expedition. Apparently he did not want to travel east either. All the first passage he simulated sickness, groaned, and lay down on the tundra, and not only did no work, but was a great nuisance to everybody. I offered to return him with his two daughters to the western shore of the Koluima River to take care of our reindeer there and he agreed with apparent pleasure.

The second Lamut, Semen, had his wife, two daughters, and a boy. At the tower camp I learned that both girls were very young and the boy had just passed the suckling age. All three were useless burdens on the expedition, as their care would take all the attention of their mother and keep her from our work. Besides that, the mother was pregnant and in a month or so we could expect to have another member added to the expedition. After a lengthy, difficult parley I succeeded in getting rid of this family, keeping only its head, Semen. I persuaded Alexey to take the wife and children with him to the western side of the Koluima River. The family itself I bribed with a sack, almost a hundred pounds, of dried bread and twenty-five rubles in cash.

The third family, childless Nicklas and Uliana, I hired at Sukharnoye and found them the best kind of workers, especially the woman. Participation of native women in such expeditions as ours was very important, really necessary, because, according to custom, almost all camp work was done by women. Especially important in the repairing and drying of all clothes and footwear, which is done by the native women, not only for their husbands, brothers, or sons, but for all male members of the expedition. During the travel itself, women work right along with the men, even to driving the baggage caravan, a job that usually fell to a woman.

11

THE REINDEER CHUKCHI

WE BEGAN to work on July sixth, more than six weeks later than we had planned. I would not say that it was a particularly successful day, chiefly because the various sections of the expedition were not working sufficiently in accord with each other. They permitted themselves to correct orders which I had given and did not follow my instructions.

Our night camp was fixed on the Medvyezhya River. All fifteen horses were heavily loaded and the reindeer caravan also bore packs, so we managed to move everything at once, although the members of the expedition, grooms, and Lamuts went forward on foot. Along the shore I walked with Kozhevnicov, examining outcrops as he surveyed. Weber went with the horse caravan to the ford over the Medvyezhya River a few miles from the sea. Unfortunately, Melnicov, who was still with us, suggested that Weber go with him in his boat to the Medvyezhya River, and Weber, tempted by this offer, accepted it. In spite of my instruction that while traveling an astronomer must never separate himself from his chronometers, he sent ahead the chronometer box with the horse caravan, and when he arrived at the meeting place after a great delay, three of the six chronometers had stopped. With the horses was only the Cossack Domashonkin, who tried to play the chief in Weber's absence.

During my travels I made a rule that if conditions for a crossing were favorable we were always to cross a river on the shore of which we expected to camp. Such instruction was given Weber's and Rumyanzev's caravans. Since our horses and reindeer were not particularly congenial, we found it more convenient to let the caravans go separately, even when they could follow the same road. Rumyanzev, therefore, led with the reindeer; he crossed the Medvyeskya River and stopped on the right shore. The horse caravan, however, did not cross the river and even turned from the ford toward the seaward shore to meet Kozhevnicov and me. They explained, in response to my reprimands, that they were afraid we might become lost. As a result, after using the Arctic summer night to move and work, on the morning of July seventh, we encamped in two sections about three miles from each other with the river between.

While walking with Kozhevnicov along the shore to the meeting place, we passed Syedov's camp. With his assistant Jucov and his crew, Syedov was settled very comfortably in a small storehouse on the sea shore. His work was proceeding very well; he had already constructed a number of beacons on the shore of the continent and neighboring islands. Syedov visited us the day we encamped on the Medvyezhya River, as the bad weather did not permit him to continue his work. He was particularly welcomed because of the opportunity his visit gave us to compare with Syedov's the three chronometers that had stopped on the previous day. It was our last meeting until I saw him in St. Petersburg the next spring.

Near Laptev's Tower, north of it and farther east toward the Medvyezhya River along the ocean, the shore was everywhere rocky, built of various slates and eruptive diabasic rocks which outcropped in the Cape Medvyezhi, protruding into the sea just on the eastern side of the embouchure of the Koluima River. The shore was not higher than two or three scores of feet, but very interesting on account of its perfectly leveled surface. There is no certain proof that sea activity produced this level surface, but it is difficult to account for such a surface otherwise.

The embouchure of the Koluima River and the seacoast in the vicinity were covered with an enormous quantity of driftwood. Here and there we saw first-grade beams, which probably had drifted from the very sources of the Koluima. The long transportation by river and the waves of the sea had shorn large trees of branch and bark. Considering how little driftwood a river carries and how much of it is deposited on the river shores, accumulations of the size which we saw in the mouth of the Koluima River are surprising. Undoubtedly the work of a great many years, such accumulations were possible only in the Arctic climate. In southern seas, where decaying processes go on through the whole year in a very intensive way, driftwood well soaked with water would rot and be destroyed much more quickly than under conditions of the Arctic climate.

During the night of July seventh a sudden wind shift brought bad weather. The river rose and the ford was no longer passable. On the eighth of July we were still separated from our Lamuts in the reindeer caravan. Not until the following day was a crossing possible. The fifteen horses swam the stream, their loads transported in several trips by *cayuk*.

Beginning at the Medvyezhya River, in a number of temporary settlements we found Reindeer Chukchi, who in summer lived along the sea coast. Their large, spherical leather tents or *yerangas* were everywhere, on the sea coast itself, at the embouchures of rivers, along the bights, and on the shores of numerous lakes in the coastal tundra. We also frequently met herds of reindeer, thousands of well-fed animals in great contrast to our invalids. I was told by Russians that Chukchi sell their reindeer most unwillingly, even when offered good payment, but after great difficulty I succeeded in buying a few animals.

I visited a Chukcha who was ready to sell me a reindeer for twenty rubles. With Melnicov for an interpreter, we were received in a very friendly manner and treated with tea and meat rather palatably fried on the skillet. I gave the host twenty silver rubles. After a while he told Melnicov that he would like to be paid more. Translating it, Melnicov told me that such was the custom here and I should have to add something. I answered that I intended to follow my own customs, and if the man would not sell the reindeer for the fixed price, I would request the return of the money. Melnicov was scared and tried to persuade me to be more lenient, but I turned directly to the host and told him to return the money. The host insisted while Melnicov tried to persuade me that without something extra it would be impossible to get anywhere. I repeated, "Money back," and at last everything was ended to my satisfaction. I noticed, however, that the host was a little surprised by such a stubborn Russian. I later observed that such extortion was not practiced in transactions between Chukchi living near the Bering Strait and American or Russian traders.

Another Chukcha sold me two reindeer for forty rubles. He did not want money but demanded a Berdana rifle and ammunition. It was a bargain because for such a rifle I paid three rubles, and perhaps twice as much for a box of ammunition. The trouble was that I had given the last Berdana to my Lamuts, who had no arms other than knives. Now it was necessary to take the rifle back from them and give it to the owner of the reindeer, to his complete satisfaction.

With much greater ease than we bought the reindeer, we purchased several sledges and reindeer harness, of which we were very short. The Medvyezhya was the last place where we could pay for our purchases in cash, always in silver rubles. Reindeer Chukchi whom we met there were familiar with Russian money from their transactions with Russians during the fair at Panteleikha. I soon found, however, that when they wished to buy something from us and pay with money, their ideas about the real value of a ruble became rather vague.

The most familiar money unit here is a brick of tea or

tobacco put up in uniform bundles. Tea bricks are manufactured in both known varieties of tea, green and black. The bricks are made by compressing about two and a half pounds of tea leaves and dust. The black brick is about twelve inches long, eight inches wide, and one inch thick; the green brick is larger. Tea bricks are very hard; only with a knife is it possible to take off the chips. Green bricks are used by Mongols, Buryats, and Russians of Transbaicalia, where the brick chips are boiled with milk and seasoned with salt. When the milk is brought to the boiling point, the mixture is stirred, and the result is a very palatable and nutritive drink, as I can confirm from personal experience. Roasted flour and butter added to the green tea prepared with milk transform the drink into a regular meal.

Black bricks are used throughout Siberia in the same way as a regular black tea of low grade. During the manufacturing process, certain trademarks are stamped on the bricks. A very common and widely known mark was a Chinese character, more or less corresponding in its outline to the shape of a spruce tree. Chukchi, who are extremely conservative and narrow-minded, always required "spruce bricks," considering all others of low quality and, therefore, of lesser value. After a while, however, as there appeared on the market different kinds of tea bearing diverse trademarks, often merely the names of Russian firms, "spruce bricks" became less common, and the Chukchi paid more attention to the good qualities of the tea bricks than to their trademarks. If the sides and, particularly, the angles of a brick became rounded, which easily happened during transportation, its value decreased, just as a gold coin depreciates below its face value when it becomes worn.

Tobacco, another barter object in northern Siberia, belonged to a variety grown in southern Russia. It had a very pungent odor and a strong taste. Used almost exclusively for pipes, it was sometimes mixed with pine bark. Tobacco is sent to market in bundles of full leaves, about a pound to the bundle. A bundle with rather loose leaves not broken off on the edges was equal in value to a brick of tea. Broken leaves or somewhat rounded bundles were of lesser value.

Tea and tobacco were asked in barter all along the coast to the Bering Strait, for neither items were delivered by American traders. I knew, however, that beginning at Shelgaski Cape it would be necessary for us to pay for different services with furs, particularly with skins of ice foxes which natives collected for trade with Americans. We also needed furs for winter garments of which in the future we would require more than we already had. We realized also, to my great and unpleasant surprise, that our Lamuts had come to the expedition very scantily clad and we were forced to clothe as well as to feed them. As the result of all these conditions, we had to begin immediately to supply the expedition with furs intended for future barter, and for our clothing. Furs for the latter purpose had to be tanned and then garments made whenever an opportunity presented itself. I was very glad to begin such barter at our first camp, for it gave us a chance to lighten our burden somewhat by exchanging a certain number of heavy tea bricks for furs.

Kozhevnicov carried on all trade and did it with great skill, appearing to find pleasure in talking trade with the Chukchi. Among them were men who specialized in trading for reindeer, for dogs, and for harnesses of different kinds; no woman would even talk about trading for these items. Such commodities as ice foxes, skin of reindeer, and seals were also in the care of men. Women dealt chiefly with cheap skins. They brought skins from reindeer legs for fur boots, skins of young calves who had died almost immediately after birth (the deaths occurring chiefly on account of unfavorable weather conditions), and tendons from the backbone of reindeer, from which threads are made for sewing furs. Ready-made objects such as gloves, socks, boots, hats, bags made of whole seal skin—everything manufactured by women—were also their merchandise.

Prices required by men for their commodities were more or less fixed, and were regulated by the prices in the eastern part of the peninsula, which in turn were regulated by American traders. The barter choices of the men were rather limited and we could easily control their wishes. If, for example, one man wanted his price in full in tobacco, to avoid running short of any commodity at the very beginning of travel, we would offer to pay him partly in tea and usually he would accept. Some wished to trade for dried bread or sugar, but since we had neither in great excess, we usually offered an acceptable substitute. Women were inclined to trade for a greater variety of items. Much of their merchandise was cheap; very few things in their possession would bring a brick of tea or a bundle of tobacco. Women did not like a quick sale but preferred to sell piece by piece. Kozhevnicov not only opened boxes containing many attractive things before their eyes, but he understood very well how to exhibit those attractions in ways most appealing to Chukchi women.

On the Medvyezhya River our expedition was at last in shape and its routine established. Besides myself, Kozhevnicov, and Weber, we had two grooms (Yakut Mitrophan and a Russian village elder, Shculev) and an interpreter, Rumyanzev, who was of mixed origin. He called himself a Yacuguir, but had in his veins some Russian blood and some Chukchi as well—at least on our travel he met Chukchi who claimed to be his relatives. There were also the Cossack Domashonkin and seven Lamuts, six men and one woman.

Melnicov left us at this camp. He had worked hard since the time when I met him on the Koluima River, but his work had a typical bureaucratic character and, although I could have kept him with us, I was glad to let him go. He did what was required of him but cared nothing about the quality of his work. He had purchased poor reindeer for us, and he had hired Lamuts who were almost useless for the purposes of our expedition and whom I kept only because we had no others. The groom he hired was so unsatisfactory that I sent him back with Melnicov. The very poor Cossack Domashonkin was Melnicov's protégé, as I learned later. A few workmen whom I had picked up myself proved of a much better grade. Melnicov lacked authority among the natives and, as was typical of Russian officials in the Koluima District, he was afraid of the Chukchi. But, no matter what I thought about it, Melnicov himself appreciated his work very highly and valued his service accordingly.

We had two tents, a small one for me and a larger one where Kozhevnicov and Weber lived and which also served as the living, dining, and reception room. Receptions were an unavoidable part of our travel. At all camps we had to serve tea with dried bread and sugar to visitors who were anxious to come into our tent to look at our paraphernalia and observe us. We were surprised and annoyed by the behavior of the Chukchi. They came into the tents whenever they wished to, often when there was no free room at all; apparently they were surprised when several times we showed them out in order to work or to be left alone, and when I flatly refused to let them come into my tent they were offended. My Koluima people also thought such a rule not quite right, perhaps even somewhat dangerous. I told them, however, that I would be master at my camp, that I was ready to offer the natives all the hospitality in our power, but I would not permit them to overrun us. Very soon we noticed that our visitors became less annoying, perhaps because of my rule, perhaps because gradually they lost interest in us.

Our Lamuts slept in a leather tent similar in shape to the *yerangas* of the Chukchi but of much smaller dimensions. Russian workmen used the *polog*, a small tent of almost cubic form made of a cotton fabric, which gave some protection against wind, rain, and, most important, mosquitoes.

Our work proceeded in this way: I left a camp on

deerback and, accompanied by a Lamut and a reindeer loaded with instruments and collections, followed the shore line with excursions to the mountains near the shore. Usually I rode less than I walked. My man was following me, waiting for me or going ahead, as suited the conditions. Unfortunately his lack of interest in our work, or negligence and laziness, often made our meetings somewhat uncertain and caused us to lose time. Once when I was in need of some instrument and hurried from the hillside near the shore to my reindeer, I saw my man about half a mile ahead and still going. I could neither make him hear me nor could I overtake him. He was ambling along quite close to the edge of the perfectly smooth water so I took my rifle and sent several bullets into water as close to the Lamut as I could without endangering him. The sudden splashes of bullets attracted his attention and he came back to me. This small incident created for me a reputation as a marksman, which probably helped us later.

Kozhevnicov followed the shore line with another Lamut and a sledge on which he used to seat himself perhaps even less frequently than I on my reindeer. Sometimes, when we knew that the road along the shore would be barely passable, we used reindeer only for baggage. Often our progress was hampered by the rivulets which flowed into the ocean. All of them were small but many were too deep to be forded and in such cases we had to order our *cayuk*, which was carried on a sledge with the reindeer caravan, to the embouchure of the river. When we expected several crossings on the same day, we ordered the caravan to follow us, but this apparently simple operation was seldom done smoothly and sometimes we waited hours for our small boat. Horses in the charge of our grooms traveled close to the shore line, deviating from it only when it was necessary to look for fords across rivulets and creeks often impassable near their mouths.

The reindeer caravan, in Weber's charge, traveled rather far from the shore, using the wet grassy tundra for a road and crossing numerous creeks near their sources where it was usually very shallow or there were good fording places. The reindeer caravan moved very slowly not only because of the sometimes rather long detours, but also on account of the poor conditions of our animals and the very low mentality of our crew. Our Lamuts were paupers, who possessed hardly any reindeer of their own and very little experience in the work which was entrusted to them. They carried on their business with more apathy and negligence than I had ever observed among natives. Unfortunately Weber could not influence them to do better work, for he had no experience of his own and could not acquire any while traveling under such conditions. In all his orders he followed the advice and instructions of the Cossack Domashankin, a man of a very low character with exactly the same psychological make-up as the Lamuts.

Living in the Chukchi area under the influence of the latter, Lamuts accepted and supported only Chukchi standards. Since Chukchi never travel in summer, Lamuts thought summer sledge travel with reindeer was some kind of profanation. This fact may account for the driving away of our reindeer on the left shore of the Koluima River, and the mysterious disappearance of Soloviev's shepherd with our animals. The Lamuts gave no thought to the special conditions of summer travel, but did everything as it would be done in winter, with results destructive to harness as well as to our low, light Chukchi sledges. Although a good reindeer driver is able to make repairs to his sledge in case of emergency, our Lamuts were lacking in this ability and frequently we had to buy new sledges to maintain the transportation capacity of the caravan. New harness was necessary also, as well as frequent repairs to the old. Often I was forced to help and even to teach the Lamuts how to mend harness.

In the very beginning I learned that for summer travel over tundra our Lamuts were using only one reindeer for every sledge. It would have been impossible for strong, fresh animals to draw the load easily and I was quite upset when I saw how our poor animals were straining, using their last strength to pull loaded sledges over grass and sand, between bumps and holes. My orders to harness at least two reindeer to a sledge met with strong opposition. Lamuts told me that we had not enough gear for such double harnessing, that the sledges were constructed differently from those which I had previously used, that their reindeer, not trained for such a double harnessing, would be unmanageable. But when we found more leather straps, ordered new harness, and made supplementary parts for sledges which permitted us to harness two reindeer to one sledge, the animals did not protest. Without that change it is quite possible that the strength of our animals would have been exhausted during the first few days of travel.

None of the Lamuts had a strong liking for the expedition, but only one of them deserted. On the fifth night in camp, one Lamut did not appear. Next morning I collected all the Lamuts and told them in a very formal way how seriously John (the name of the fugitive) had harmed himself. He would live now outlawed everywhere. I told them also that if, by chance, I should witness a similar runaway, I would stop the fugitive with my rifle. My reputation as a marksman was already well established at that time and the natives attributed some mysterious properties to my rifle, a Russian army rifle unknown in northern Siberia. Among Chukchi a rumor circulated that with this rifle I could kill enchanted people immune against the iron (nickel-covered) bullet of the best American Winchester. The next day the fugitive arrived at the camp with the explanation that on the previous evening he had fallen asleep in the tundra. I pretended to believe the tale.

In planning the expedition I had expected that the topographical and geological survey would go more slowly than the caravans of our main expeditionary body. In practice, however, Kozhevnicov and I proceeded to the night camping place along with the horses of the expedition, or immediately after. The reindeer caravan was always late and once we waited for it exactly twelve hours, which was most inconvenient, for without the necessary materials in the reindeer caravan we could not begin some of the night camp work. At almost every camp we had to dry our baggage after the travel over wet tundra on low sledges. But we were moving and working, although our reindeer were at the point of exhaustion. My hopes were centered now in Soloviev's herd, which was still ahead of us. We almost overtook the shepherd east of the Bolshoi Baranov Cape where, according to information received from Chukchi, he had camped not so long ago. He moved, however, farther eastward immediately after he had learned of our approach.

We overtook him near the Konyechnaya River. Our meeting was a bitter disappointment for me because the twenty reindeer which we received from Soloviev's shepherd were also in very poor shape. My Russians had an idea that it was a trick of the shepherd, nicknamed Secretary because of a crafty character which reminded people of Russian officials. It was suspected that Secretary exchanged with Chukchi our good reindeer for poor ones. My Russian workmen did not suffer from rich imaginations and probably they had heard something about such an affair. I never could quite decide whether or not Soloviev was partly involved in this conspiracy. We were losing reindeer practically every day. Several of the reindeer received from Secretary perished during the first days. We also lost a horse. I tried to utilize condemned reindeer for food, killing them when they could not work. We consumed a reindeer in two or three days, but after several meals of this kind my Russian workmen told me that if I did not give them better meat they would eat exclusively with the Chukchi, depending on the hospitality of the latter. Frankly, I could not blame them, because the meat of an exhausted reindeer has a very poor, somewhat raggish texture and a nauseating odor.

The shore changed its appearance east of the Medvyezhya River where the Mali Baranov Cape, a flat-topped hill about a thousand feet high, is separated from mountains which rise a few miles south of the coast and attain an altitude of at least two or three thousand feet. Between these mountains and the Mali Baranov Cape spread a low drift land only a few scores of feet above sea level. A little change in the level of the sea would transform the cape into an island, which presumably it had been originally. Geologically the cape was a granitic stock intruded into slates of different petrographical character. Probably the cape had been connected formerly with the southern mountain ridges, but separated later from the mainland by the wave erosion which affected the less resistant slates more than the granite. The large stock of the latter was preserved therefore in the form of an island. I thought that the geological structure of this cape suggested the geology of the mountains in the inward continent; and later, when in Chaun Bay I was able to check this suggestion, I found it to be true. Trips into mountains and direct examination of their geology were impossible for me under our conditions of travel, so it was fortunate that, in contradiction to a well-known expression, the mountain came to the prophet by its geological similarity to the cape. The lowland around the cape was covered with lakes, swamps, and grassy tundra, and here our horse and reindeer caravans traveled. In winter, dog driving also went over these low areas. Low drift ground filled up shallow bays between the capes, which made them protrude less from the shore than the term "cape" indicates. On the coast east of Chaun Bay, areas between capes were usually occupied by large lagoons running along the shore for many miles. For some distance low land around capes could not be seen and from a sailing boat they could therefore easily be mapped as islands. One such cape, discovered near the Dezhneva Cape in the Bering Sea, appeared for a long time on navy maps as an island before it was found to be a part of the continent connected with the shore by means of very low land.

Besides the large stocks, granite was found in slates often in the form of dikes. Other dikes were of different porphyries. Being much more resistant to erosion than slates, all these dikes protruded on the slopes of rocky shores in the form of walls and towers, often of a quite fantastic shape. All these protruding masses Russians called *kekurs*. We saw a great number of them on the coast west of the Bolshoi Baranov Cape and on the slopes of the latter.

East of Bolshoi Baranov Cape the coast was composed of so-called Tundra Horizon—clays and sands deposited in deltas or lakes and soaked with water which was frozen. West of the Bolshaya River we came across the ice cliffs in which layers of so-called permanent ice were more than forty feet thick. The Tundra Horizon was well known in geological and even popular literature because in these strata were found frozen the carcasses of mammoth and rhinoceros, the flesh of which was eagerly devoured by wolves, ice foxes, and dogs. The whole shore between Bolshaya River and Chaun Bay, the Karchnik Peninsula, and Aion Island are built of the same Tundra Horizon, but we saw ice here only in small isolated pockets.

On July twenty-fifth we were at the embouchure of the Bolshaya River on Great River. Only in comparison with many small streams flowing into the Arctic Ocean was the river large. On the shore we found a house and small church, the ruins of an old Russian settlement. Two or three scores of years ago there had been a mission here.

The next goal was the embouchure of the Chaun River which entered the bay of the same name in its southern part, where we had had a depot since spring. I tried to get information about our next road into Chaun Bay around the Karchuik Peninsula. Chukchi were quite positive that this peninsula protruded toward the north much further than Wrangel, whose expedition worked here in the twenties of the last century, had indicated on his map. I could not believe the Chukchi, for we had had the opportunity to check Wrangel's work and had found it quite dependable. It was possible to expect some differences, but only insignificant ones. More serious, however, was the statement of Chukchi that pasturage was extremely bad at the northern end of the peninsula. We could not take the chance of letting reindeer in such condition as ours go for two or three days without good grass. This risk might have been permissible with strong, well-fed animals, but in our case it would mean destruction of the whole herd. At the same time our Lamuts, Chukchi, and Secretary told me that there was a direct way from the Bolshaya River to the Chaun River, which it would be possible to traverse with good reindeer in eight days. In Secretary's opinion, even with our reindeer, we could cover the route there in less than three weeks. At first he promised to be our guide and to help with his, or rather with Soloviev's reindeer, but later on he changed his mind to my great regret because, in spite of his crafty character, he was a man of enterprise and energy. Probably he did not like to work his reindeer in the summer.

I decided to send our reindeer caravan and half of the horses by this direct route to our depot on the Chaun River, appointing Weber the head of this party. He was also directed to make a topographical survey of the route with the necessary astronomical observations. I asked him also to pay some attention to the geology of the area and to bring along a few specimens of rocks which would attract his attention. For a guide he had one of our Lamuts who was familiar with this route. Kozhevnicov, Shculev, Rumyanzev, and I, all on horseback with three pack horses, were to move along the shore. Kozhevnicov as usual had to survey. Besides geological observations, I intended to make astronomical observations, for which purpose I had the reserve universal instrument with which I observed at Sredne- and Nijne-Koluimsk, one pocket chronometer and two so-called comparison watches. The latter, being not so sensitive as the chronometers to shocks unavoidable under conditions of travel similar to ours, were expected to give results comparable in their precision to the work of a pocket chronometer. To protect the watches against sharp shocks and sudden changes of temperature, I put them into a small upholstered box on pillows made of wood shavings.

I expected that Weber would arrive at Chaun before us, but had hopes that owing to our travel on horseback we would not be much later. Weber was instructed to send a messenger from Chaun to Shelgaski and to order from there one or two *biadaras*—large skin boats used by the Maritime Chukchi. I could see that with our present transportation facilities it would be impossible for us to move our depot from the Chaun River northward.

12

THE CAMP ON THE CHAUN

ON THE evening of July twenty-ninth, after Weber and I made simultaneous astronomical observations at our camp at the Bolshaya River, my small party left the camp and crossed to the other shore, using our *cayuk* to carry over the loads.

The next morning, when we were ready to leave, a Lamut arrived by *cayuk* to tell us that Chukchi who visited Weber shortly after our departure informed him that we were camping on an island. With the help of the Lamut we continued to cross the river and this time landed on its other shore. Owing to the small size of the *cayuk* we spent half a day transporting the loads; were it not for the boat we would have had to build a raft.

The trip along the shore to our depot on the Chaun River was perhaps the best part of our whole travel. Our rate of twenty miles a day was not bad, considering that we surveyed and explored during the passage. For the first time during the whole expedition I was free of troubles with our reindeer caravan, troubles more

144

tiresome than the actual work of the expedition. I felt as though I were having a vacation.

Our new routine was established very quickly. Early in the morning we were up and, after a quick breakfast, worked until eleven o'clock, the time set for luncheon. After three hours of rest for the horses, we traveled until the night camp, which we always tried to make on good grazing ground. For my companion I had Shculev, in whose care was the horse that carried the chronometers. Where the shore was rocky with many outcrops, I let Shculev have my horse while I walked. With Kozhevnicov was Rumyanzev, who had in his care two pack horses.

As I thought, the discrepancy between Wrangel's survey of the Karchuik Peninsula and ours was not so great as one might have expected from stories told by the natives. Rather unexpectedly, however, we ran across a number of temporary settlements of Reindeer Chukchi, whose herds were grazing at the northern end of the peninsula. All those stories about poor grass were pure invention in which, perhaps, our own reindeer people had some share.

Karchuik Peninsula, as well as the neighboring shore of the Arctic Ocean, was composed of loose Post-Pliocene sands and clays, mostly frozen, of the Tundra Horizon, with layers of permanent ice in many places. Such frozen ground is not only easily eroded by running water, but during warm weather the ground itself begins to flow. A great amount of sand and clay is carried in that manner into the sea and deposited there in the form of dangerous shoals, sometimes at a great distance from the shore, making navigation along that part of the coast immediately west of Chaun Bay more dangerous than anywhere else between the Koluima River and Bering Strait. After our return we warned the marine service, but the subsequent grounding of two Russian steamers off that strip of coast indicated that little heed had been given our warning. Even on the shore the mud streams flowing from the frozen ground were dangerous. Vollossovitch, the leader of the western party of the expedition, told me that he tried once to cross such a mud stream and was caught by the sticky mud from which he could be freed only with the help of his workmen, who fortunately were not far off. When he examined the place the next morning, he found that his footprints of the previous day had been frozen, indicating what would have happened to his feet and, of course, to himself, if he had not been rescued.

Because of the geology of the Karchuik Peninsula even the small rivers were practically impassable for us near their mouths. All of them flowed quietly without rapids, and had, therefore, a uniform depth, but there were no well-marked fords because the water was usually muddy and most of the stream bottoms dirty and sticky. The rivulets had cut quite deep channels between low, but steep, almost vertical banks which horses could descend only with difficulty. At first we tried to cross one of these rivers at the lower part of its embouchure or beyond the mouth, looking for a bar. When running water loaded with silt comes into contact with stagnant sea water, it immediately begins to deposit the suspended materials. Usually the fine silt is transported a long distance from the shore, but the sand is deposited much closer, forming a bar at the mouth of the river. Not only is the water over the bar shallower than the river itself, but the bar forms a hard sandy bottom. The search for such a bar sometimes took us half a mile or more out into the sea, but this was possible only when the sea was calm. Sometimes we were lucky enough to cross a river in that way, but many times we failed to find a sand bar and had to go up the river looking for a ford. After that, we returned to the sea again along the opposite shore in anticipation of a possible repetition of the detour a few miles farther on. Once it took two days to make such a detour.

For night camping in the tundra it was necessary to carry driftwood, which was found abundantly everywhere along the shore. In sheltered places, such as the western shore of Chaun Bay which was protected from the northern winds by Aion Island, driftwood was scarce. Our forced trips into tundras were annoying, for they took much time and curtailed our progress along the shore, but we saw the tundras better than would have been possible from the sea shore. We found the peninsula well populated and several big herds of reindeer pastured near large lakes. Once we called on a settlement and got some meat, our supplies of which we had just exhausted. There I was told that on Aion Island, which we had not explored, were Reindeer Chukchi in many temporary settlements along the shores as well as in the center of the island where, contrary to rumor, the pasturage was good.

The Chukchi in the area came mostly from the inner

part of Chukchi Peninsula and only infrequently met Russians. Many of them had never been on the Koluima River nor had they traveled to the east where they could see Americans. Once, sitting at tea with a number of Chukchi, I noticed that one of them looked at us with great curiosity. He told our interpreters that he was looking at Russians for the first time in his life.

Because of their isolation, the primitive nature of these natives was unspoiled. They were not so annoying as the Chukchi of the Medvyezhya; they were rather polite, and ready to help us when they could. Twice they saved us long detours by taking us across rivers in their skin boats. Apparently they had not heard about the expedition, but once or twice they mentioned something about robbers and criminals and told us that our sudden appearance had scared them. To my regret, I did not learn whether their fears had any connection with the Turukhansk exiles.

Many of the Chukchi had never seen horses before and how they admired and feared the big animals! They were particularly surprised by the amount and size of horse dung. Several times I saw a Chukcha watching for the moment when a horse was ready to relieve himself. He looked under the tail and followed the process from beginning to end. *"Haccome!"* exclaimed he, expressing with this untranslatable exclamation akin to the American "My! My!" his surprise and delight. To get our horses across the Kusimina River and to make sure they did not run away as soon as they reached the shore, we tied two horses to three others, thereby hampering their movements, and let them swim across the river in two groups. A Chukcha carried me to the other shore in his small *baidara*. I watched the swimming horses and as soon as they were close to the shore I jumped into the water, grasped the bridles of both groups to get them under control before they touched ground, and then pulled both to the shore. Then I called to the Chukcha to take care of one group while I disposed of the other. No answer; no action. I looked around and could not see the man anywhere. While I stood waiting patiently for my people who were crossing the river with the two remaining horses and our baggage on a raft, I saw the Chukcha crawl out from under a pile of driftwood, still fearful of the terrible brutes and by no means ready to give me any help.

The low shore of the Karchuik Peninsula along the strait that separates Aion Island from the continent gave Kozhevnicov a regular headache. Along the Arctic shore, waves and currents caried away and deposited their load of sediments some distance from the shore. The line of the latter was therefore well defined. In the shallow strait between Aion Island and the continent such a carrying-away of sediment did not take place. As a result, the shore was very low and covered with water or mud, depending upon a change of even a few inches of water level which might be brought about by a wind. At the time of our passage, the water in the bay was low, and we drove for a long distance over cracked ground white with dried-out salt. Elevations a few inches above that lifeless surface were covered with grass. With a slight rise of water they would become small green islands. At times we were lost among small and large lakes, arms of water, inlets, and wide swamps. Fluctuation of the shore line for a distance of a mile or two almost made a nervous wreck of Kozhevnicov. A dotted line indicating the shore was the solution of our problem. Fortunately we worked on the Karchuik Peninsula during very good weather, or our troubles with tundra rivers would have been much greater. Good clear weather allowed me to make two astronomical determinations along our route, both times in the tundra. Under the warm noonday sun it was extremely difficult to keep the instrument immobile on the frozen ground. Only by constructing a kind of floor of long beams for the tripod and staying during the observation between the beams, was it possible to make somewhat dependable observations.

All our troubles with dirty tundra rivers were over when we followed the western shore of Chaun Bay over the slope of Kaim Hill, built of slates cut through with different porphyries, where the cliffs were rocky and rivers swift and shallow with gravel bottoms. However, on the elevated rocky slope of Kaim Hill we found poor pasturage for our horses, and one night were forced to keep them tied. On a poor grass, even fettered horses do not remain long at the same place, but wander all night, often for several miles, looking for a better pasturage.

After we had passed Kaim Hill we came again to low shores along the southern part of Chaun Bay and again found a number of temporary settlements of the Reindeer Chukchi, some of whom had happened to visit our depot on the Chaun River. These Chukchi proved very helpful to us. One of them, Emancov, accompanied by his step-son, immediately joined us in two small *baidaras*. When we came to a river flowing into the bay, they both helped us to find a ford. If a river was too deep, they took us over with our loads. Since the Chaun River enters the bay in several arms, without the help of the Chukchi it would have been necessary for us to go up the river to look for a ford beyond the delta area. When I worked on the cliffs or forded around small capes protruding into the bay, these Chukchi watched all my movements from their *baidaras*. At the camps they were regular workmen who did everything and helped in everything except the managing of horses. Their services were offered quite free and none of them mentioned a remuneration at any time. The only thing I gave them was the food which we shared with them.

The trip around Chaun Bay was very important to us for it gave a good insight into the geology of the mountains filling all this area. Such outcrops as observed in the Kaim Hill and in other places showed that the coastal capes corresponded completely in their geological structure to mountains, and undoubtedly were actually isolated parts of the latter. In Kaim Hill, and later on the eastern shore of the bay in Razsomachi Cape, mountains approached shores directly.

On August sixteenth we camped for the night on the shore of the Chaun River and in the morning of the next day were at our depot on the eastern shore of the river. Here I met two new members of the expedition, the Cossack Kipriyanov and the interpreter Berejnov. Both had arrived with our supplies and were waiting for the expedition without any idea of where we were or when we should arrive. When they were sent to the Chaun they were told that the expedition would arrive there at the beginning of summer. As a matter of fact, the vanguard of the expedition did not arrive until the end of summer. Kipriyanov was weak and broken in health, but even so he was much better than the Cossack Domashonkin. The other fellow, Berejnov, was found later to be the best man of the party. As an interpreter he was excellent, with a perfect command of the Chukchi language and the ability to translate it into good Russian. He was a good companion and the interests of the expedition soon became his own.

Since, contrary to our plans, we arrived before Weber, we had to hire at Shelagski Cape one or two *baidaras* to move our baggage toward the north. The Chukcha, Emancov, was ready to be our messenger, and I hired for him a companion among the Reindeer Chukchi who dwelt in *yerangas* near our depot. Emancov left for this long and difficult trip without asking for remuneration.

While we waited for our caravan we began our preparation for winter travel by trading with Chukchi, as before with Kozhevnicov in the position of chief salesman. I was lucky enough to purchase several skins of young reindeer four or five months old, which make the best fur for winter clothes. I also found chamois skin in sufficient amount to make a *chum*, the conical tent used by Tungus and Yakuts, which is quite similar in shape to the wigwam of the North American Indians. The leather tents of Lamuts and the *yerangas* of Chukchi are of very different dimensions, but they have the same hemispherical form. The conical *chum* had a smaller volume than even the smallest *yeranga*, but could accommodate three people very well.

Owing to its smaller volume, the *chum* was easily heated by means of a small iron stove which we had brought along. A *chum* was easier to handle than a tent. To set up a tent it was always necessary to use several stakes, and to drive them into frozen ground was always a very difficult task, at times impossible on ice, though ice surface is very convenient for camping. There are no stakes in a *chum*; the high sticks which form the skeleton are simply arranged on the ground in the form of a cone. Even a strong wind does not affect such a conical structure except perhaps to tear off its leather cover. Wrapping the cover with leather straps helps in such an emergency. From the standpoint of ventilation, the *chum* is superior. A tent in the polar regions very soon becomes wet inside and rime covers the walls. When the cover is hot, the rime melts and water soaks the linen, which, when frozen, requires extreme care in unpacking. The chamois skin of a *chum* is always dry and soft. Several Chukchi women took orders to sew skins, under my direction, for the cover of our future home. We had trouble in procuring twelve sticks about twelve feet long from our only source of lumber, driftwood. When we found suitable beams, we split them and cut the sticks to proper thickness and shape with our knives.

For the transportation of all our supplies from the depot, we had another packing job at hand. I have mentioned already the big boxes in which our goods had been packed. The opening of the boxes alone required much time and hard work. We found some workers among the Chukchi who loafed at our camp all the time, but it was extremely difficult to explain to them what we wanted. The simplest piece of work for us was a real problem for them; they could go on with a job only when it had been done before their eyes to the point where its purpose and meaning were clear. I was in danger of becoming a regular slave driver of our Russian workmen, but without a direct command they did not do anything. If they were not watched they managed to sneak out to the Chukchi quarters and lie down there. Shculev and Rumyanzev might consider camping on the Chaun River as some sort of vacation after a trip of almost three weeks, but Berejnov and Kipriyanov had been idle for over three months and I could not understand why they were not tired of such a long inactivity. I was very anxious to finish our work as soon as possible for, while we could not expect an early delivery of the *baidaras* which Emancov would order, others might arrive unexpectedly any day. It was the time of year when Chukchi from the Shelagski Cape came to the Chaun River to get supplies of meat and reindeer skins from the Reindeer Chukchi. We should be prepared for their arrival.

Among other work, I had to watch for favorable moments for astronomical observations. The weather was very changeable. A bright sun favoring observations would shine only to be covered in a few minutes; a cloudy day for a brief while would suddenly become sunny, so that it was necessary to keep our instrument ready for observation and have an astronomer available at all times. I had no opportunity to do geological work. The depot was located on the drift land and I could not travel far away from it, because the horses had been left on the western shore of the river, and the only *baidara*, Emancov's, had been taken by him on his trip to the Shelagski Cape. The lack of boats also prevented me from making a trip up the river.

On August eighteenth Emancov's step-son arrived in his little *baidara*. He had traveled with us a few days, but had left us to bring from his herd a few reindeer which I had bought from him. He told us that our caravan would arrive the next day. One of our Lamuts, Paul, had intended to come with him, but because of a strong wind the two could not sail over the river in a small *baidara*, and so Paul had returned to his companions. The next day came and passed, then several days more, with no news about Weber and his caravan. On August twenty-fourth, looking through my field glass I noticed on the western shore of the river, about six miles from the depot, a high mast with a flag on top. After a while we saw on the sea shore of the island in front of the depot a man riding on a reindeer. He carried a flag in his hand. It was the Lamut, Paul, who had been sent by Weber "to look for the depot." Weber arrived that evening.

They had come to the southern shore of Chaun Bay on August fourteenth, shortly after us. From there the Lamuts decided to take the "direct" road over the tundra. Quite purposelessly they wandered on the western shore of the river for four days and then announced to Weber that they were without hope of ever finding us. Weber immediately gave the order to erect a signal and sent Paul out with a flag. Every native in the party knew exactly where our depot was. All their wandering, their despair at not finding us, was nothing else than a desire to fool Weber. I was at a loss at first to understand the reasons for the whole comedy, but soon Weber shed light on the play. The Lamuts had told him that they would not go farther than the Chaun and from the western shore of the river would turn back to the Koluima River. They were afraid of the approaching winter on the Arctic shore and feared that the reindeer would not have any food there. Domashonkin had increased their fears by repeatedly telling them that we expected to travel to America and that our people would be left somewhere on the coast with no consideration for their fate. Behind all the intrigue was the desire of Domashonkin to leave for home as soon as possible. He could not go alone and for that reason worked on the Lamuts.

During the travel from the Bolshaya River it was easy for Domashonkin to interfere with Weber's arrangements and orders because Weber could not order anything without the interpreter. Since Weber had had no experience in travel, he could not be critical of the advice of his assistant who apparently was bent upon showing to the Lamuts that the head of the party did not know anything about traveling, in that way undermining very successfully the authority of his boss and of all of us. I decided to go to the Lamuts' camp and break the revolt at any price. With Berejnov to interpret I went over and found to my surprise that the Lamuts seemed quite friendly and sincerely glad to see me, although they had been acting like children scared by the stupid tales of their nurse. My talk was much easier than I had anticipated. I congratulated the Lamuts on their happy arrival and expressed my pleasure that all of them were all right, concluding with some remarks concerning my appreciation of their work—the last not quite sincere. I told them that I was giving them a free day and did not expect them to cross the river to the depot before the next day. This, I noticed, upset them, and when Domashonkin, who understood immediately that his achievements were in danger, started to "interpret," I sent him away and carried on further conversation exclusively through Berejnov. One of the Lamuts told me that they expected to be allowed to return home from the Chaun River. I asked who was particularly anxious to leave. Nobody was. After that we talked quite peacefully about our future plans. I told them that I expected them to go as far as the embouchure of the Verkon River and from there I would send them back. I told them that I had not forgotten their need of winter clothes, which of course was true. In such a way everything was fixed. Domashonkin, however, did not like to lose out, and that same night he began to play the man prostrated by sickness. He screamed all the time; he pretended he could not move at all and had Lamuts carry him from their tent on a reindeer skin when he wanted to go out. Unfortunately we had at our disposal very small boats which would hold two people only under exceptionally favorable conditions. In our boats we could not ferry Domashonkin across to the camp and we could not leave him alone. I could hardly refrain from giving him a good thrashing.

Next day the big *baidaras* from Shelagski Cape arrived and our situation changed at once. We spent almost the whole day ferrying reindeer, horses, and baggage, losing four sledges, one reindeer, and a few pieces of baggage. The two *baidaras* were large enough to hold all our load and I planned to transport our baggage in that way as far eastward as Yacan Cape if conditions were at all favorable. I was ready to take a chance with our two Cossacks, far from dependable people, and to send them ahead with the luggage. I had hoped that they would find some means of moving our baggage or parts of it further eastward while we would follow them. I could not, however, persuade the Chukchi to take the loads further than Shelagski Cape. All Chukchi were of the opinion that sailing east of the cape that year was impossible or very risky for their leather *baidaras*, on account of the abundance of broken ice driven to shore by the northern winds which had blown steadily during the last few days.

For the larger *baidara* I paid fifteen tea bricks and ten bundles of tobacco; for the smaller one ten tea bricks, several yards of red cotton cloth (enough to make a *kukhlynaka* or loose garment worn by Chukchi and Russians over the fur clothes for the purpose of protecting the fur against rain or wet snow), and an iron kettle. We promised also to barter some ice foxes for tea at Rautan Island and to give each of the owners of *baidaras* a bottle of vodka after everything was delivered. Our free helper, Emancov, also was given a half bottle as a well-deserved reward, on which he immediately became intoxicated.

As many people do, Emancov liked to show that he was drunk by walking noisily around provoking envy in his friends who had not such a happiness. One of them, an old fellow, had something against Emancov and, provoked now by the boasting of the latter, he spoke rather sharply to our man. Chukchi have the reputation of being self-controlled people, but I was surprised to observe how deeply such a self-control could be rooted. Emancov was younger, hence, according to the code of Chukchi, he had to take all verbal and physical insults from the older man without resistance or objection. The old fellow soon cooled, but after a while he raised the noise again, this time in the neighborhood of my tent. I called Berejnov and ordered him to tell the Chukcha that I did not permit anyone to make a noise at our camp close to my tent. Berejnov carried the message, a commotion followed, and I heard Berejnov's excited voice: "He struck me, the so and so! If only we were not dependent on you, I would show you, so and so!" Every sentence Berejnov concluded with strong Russian expressions which can be neither repeated nor translated. I jumped out from the tent and saw the old Chukcha a few feet away, very angry.

I expected that he would meet my objections as he had those of Berejnov. In my right hand, under my overcoat, I held a small automatic which I was ready to use if the Chukcha struck or pushed me as he had Berejnov. Apparently not paying him any attention, I ordered the Cossack Kipriyanov to take the old man away. The Cossack, however, was barefooted, or perhaps had removed his boots intentionally in order to have an excuse not to interfere in a dangerous situation. For a few moments it was a rather tense scene. The Chukcha and I stood confronting and watching each other, with Berejnov near by watching both of us and Kipriyanov fumbling with his boots. Suddenly the Chukcha turned to Berejnov and in quite a peaceful voice said: "It is not the Chief with whom I am angry. It is the fellow over there!" He pointed at Emancov, wandering around purposelessly far from our camp, and left.

Although this was the only trouble we had with Chukchi at our depot, I learned later of a rumor on Shelagski Cape that we had had serious friction and were close to shooting. As a result of the rumor, five men left Cape Shelagski for the Chaun with the special purpose of adjusting the matter. "We are sorry for our young people who have all their life ahead of them. We are old. The best part of our life is already passed. Let us go to Chaun and die there, if necessary, at the hands of the Russians." To that effect they spoke before leaving the Shelagski Cape. With their Winchesters, they arrived at Chaun in a *baidara* along with several others from the Cape. We did not know anything about such a campaign against us, so we did not differentiate the warriors from their more peacefully inclined friends. In the friendly atmosphere at the depot they were treated as our guests and never mentioned to us their warlike intentions. I never was able to explain satisfactorily the origin of the rumor.

After I had lost any hope of persuading the Chukchi to sail east of Shelagski Cape with our baggage, and saw that I could get from them very little geographical information, I began to talk with them about the organization of our winter travel to Bering Strait. Almost all of them said that they were ready to travel with us eastward by dog teams. They even promised to finish hastily their business at the Chaun River and return home to Shelagski Cape where we should be able to contact them. For some reason, not one of them would decide anything definite outside of his home.

On August twenty-ninth we sent the reindeer caravan with Lamuts to Shelagski Cape in charge of the Cossack Kipriyanov. They had only a small baggage and I expected them to move quickly. I did not know what to do with the other Cossack, Domashonkin, who was still "sick" and lay around all the time, not taking part in any work done at the depot. I had decided to send him also to Shelagski Cape and leave him there with Chukchi during the time of our travel to Bering Strait and back, but a Lamut who had left behind a pregnant wife was permitted to return home from the Chaun, and when Domashonkin learned of his planned exile with Chukchi he asked permission to join the Lamut, stating that he would be willing to walk home. I had scarcely time to grant permission before Domashonkin recovered instantaneously, to the great astonishment of Lamuts who had nursed him as a very sick man.

Our two *baidaras* were detained for several days by very persistent and strong northwestern winds, against which they could not sail from the embouchure of the Chaun River, since it was full of shoals. It was the first of September when Weber and Berejnov, in charge of the *baidaras*, embarked for Shelagski Cape.

Kozhevnicov and I expected to go on horseback along the eastern shore of Chaun Bay with all fourteen horses and their grooms, Shculev, Rumyanzev, and Mitrophan. More than once I remarked that the expedition had been conceived under a very unlucky star. Once more I repeated it when, on the eve of Weber's departure, I learned that Shculev was sick of diarrhea complicated with vomiting. Next day his sickness grew worse and it was absolutely impossible for him to travel on horseback. Among Chukchi from Shelagski Cape were some of Shculev's intimate friends, but I could not persuade any of them to take the sick man in their *baidaras*, although I offered them all kinds of remuneration. They were afraid that Shculev would die during the trip. One or two told me quite frankly that perhaps they would take him, but that if he should grow worse they would leave him alone somewhere on the shore. I tried to leave him among our friends, the Reindeer Chukchi near the depot, but I was unable to persuade them either. For several days I tested my medical experience on Shculev. I think I tried all drugs in our medicine chest, but without any success. At last, on the fourth of September, I decided to break away, leaving Shculev in the care of Rumyanzev, who was to wait for the time when Shculev had recovered enough to be taken by Chukchi in their *baidaras*. In the case of a fatal issue, Rumyanzev was ordered to bury his friend decently and then join us at Shelagski Cape. When we left, Shculev was in such a bad condition that I had only a very slight hope of seeing him again.

13

SIBERIAN FESTIVAL

I NOW had to depend on one groom to handle four-teen horses, half of them almost wild again after fourteen days of rest at Chaun. Everywhere but in the Yakutsk Province pack horses were permitted to go free, for they would keep with the caravan even when not following the exact path. Only horses carrying loads requiring special attention, as for instance the horse carrying chronometers and other delicate instruments, were led by a groom. They were also tied to each other and led by a groom on the path in the forest or on dangerous sections of the road, but in all other cases the groom rode alone, watching the pack horses and interfering only when he saw trouble. But Yakutsk horses left free would run away, even those tamer than ours. They had to be tied together and every group of horses pulled by a groom. Besides three horses under saddles, we had eight horses with loads and three without. On the road, eleven horses were too much work for one groom, so there was nothing for me to do but to take care of four of the pack horses, leaving the other four pack horses and one free horse for Mitrophan, and two free horses for Kozhevni-

163

cov. Kozhevnicov could not manage more than two because during the trip he was engaged in surveying. I could combine, in one way or another, the work of a geologist and a groom. When I remembered what difficulties our men had met when starting the horses from Sukharnoye, I was afraid that our travel from the Chaun River would be extremely troublesome. I think that our men had the same presentiment.

Rumyanzev helped us at the depot to catch, harness, saddle, and pack the horses, each operation difficult in itself with our wild beasts. He then went along with us for about six miles. However, everything went better than we had expected. There was trouble only once, when one of my pack horses mired and began immediately to struggle. It was necessary to jump quickly out of saddle onto the head of the horse and, keeping it fast, to try to quiet it before the whole pack became infected with the same spirit. The next day we worked out our routine and everything went well. Early in the morning all three of us had to catch the horses. They were always left on pasture with forelegs bound, but in spite of that we had to do considerable running after them. We always tried to sneak out to the horses and catch them in a narrow space, doing everything as quietly as possible. One morning we noticed that two horses had lost their bonds and walked free. We did everything possible to catch them, but they had felt freedom. Suddenly they started off at full speed, following the road which we had passed the day before. The road made a large loop around the hill at the bottom of which was our camp. I ran to the top of the hill, and with my field glass saw our still galloping horses about two miles away on our road of yesterday and already partly enveloped in the fog of a cold autumn morning. We did not try to ride after them, so both horses were lost forever. Later I was told that one horse was shot by natives, another killed by wolves, both far from the place where we had lost them. When a horse was caught and harnessed, we had a brisk time while saddling and packing. Usually one of us held the head of the animal firmly, preventing it in that way from biting and kicking the people busy with saddling. The tightening of girths met with strong opposition. Every evening Mitrophan had his hands full with repairs on harness, saddles and other equipment. All camping work, including the preparation of sleeping quarters for Mitrophan, was done, therefore, by Kozhevnicov and me.

As the southeastern shore of Chaun Bay was low and composed of the sediments of the Chaun River, my geological observations did not interfere much with my groom work. Conditions changed when the shores became high and more diverse geologically. South of Razsomachi Cape we stopped for a day while I examined the outcrops north of our camp and Kozhevnicov surveyed the same part of the shore on horseback. I returned to the camp from the end point of my observations and the next day passed all the outcrops without stopping, acting as a groom only. The day following we did not have to stop at all, because we had two horses less and the others, after several days of work, had become much tamer. When I wanted to examine outcrops, I gave my saddle horse to Kozhevnicov and the pack horses to Mitrophan, and became, for a while, a geologist. Geologically, the mountains of the eastern shore of Chaun Bay corresponded closely to Kaim Hill on the western shore of the Bay and to the capes of the Arctic coast. Differences were found only in details.

Near Peveca Cape (Rautan Mountain) we saw two *baidaras* sailing from the south. One of them landed and to our pleasure Shculev, completely recovered, joined us. In the other *baidara* Rumyanzev sailed directly to Shelagski Cape, apparently without thinking of the work waiting for him in our party.

When the *baidara* with Shculev turned to the shore, I noted the ease with which the Chukchi managed their boats and sails in spite of the flat bottom construction of their *baidaras*. Our Russians from the Koluima River, whose ancestors had been good sailors, looked at Chukchi with some admiration. They were particularly mystified by the use of the rudder, because they had nothing similar to it on their Koluima boats, which they steered with a paddle.

The *baidara* carried a good load of reindeer skins and meat. The Chukchi had not taken any precautions, but had carried the meat exposed to the sunshine, and a putrid smell was noticeable ten to twenty feet away from the *baidara*. Apparently the Chukchi were not worried about that matter at all and seemed to enjoy eating the meat as though it were from a newly killed animal.

With Shculev in our party, I was released from my groom service and could give all my time to my own work. We moved now as quickly as the travel with pack horses would permit. In a few places we had to turn from the shore inland on account of rivers, but these detours were not so long as on the Karchuik Peninsula. All the rivers had hard, graveled bottoms and fording was easy. With some pleasure and pride I realized that I found fords here more quickly than my grooms, who were more at ease dealing with the dirty tundra rivers of the Karchuik Peninsula. Since leaving the depot we had had an almost uninterrupted period of warm, dry, sunny days. It was hard to believe we were close to the middle of September and within the Arctic Circle. Again the mosquitoes appeared, together with grasshoppers whose stridulation was reminiscent of southern steppes rather than Arctic tundras.

On the fifteenth of September we arrived at our new camp near the Yanragaivenyam River a few miles south of Shelagski Cape. Here we found all our baggage sent from the Chaun in *baidaras*. Near by our Lamuts were camping with reindeer. Weber had not stopped here, but had sailed to the settlement, Shelagski, located immediately south of high, rocky Cape Shelagski, which protrudes into the sea in a northwestern direction. He had already made his astronomical observations there and had even found opportunity to sail around the Cape further eastward. Unfortunately, the Chukchi, who had not liked to sail that way with our baggage, were quite right. There was too much ice near the Arctic shore for safe sailing in *baidaras*, which are nothing more than skin boats. Weber proceeded only as far as the Koiveyam River, which later became an important turning point in the course of the expedition.

Next day Kozhevnicov, with Rumyanzev for a companion, left for a survey of Shelagski Cape, and finished it the same day. Kozhevnicov considered this survey a great achievement, one which required much effort and was very difficult and dangerous. When a few days later we sent our mail to St. Petersburg, he telegraphed a special message about this achievement. I was much surprised and alarmed at the same time, as I knew that no one considered the topographic work on Shelagski Cape so very difficult. I had made the same tour when studying the geology of the Cape. I was quite certain that Kozhevnicov did not mean to exaggerate, that he was, to the contrary, sincere about the matter, and for me it was proof that he could not stand much longer the conditions under which we were forced to work and was gradually breaking down. I realized soon that I was right —Kozhevnicov's morale suffered badly. Of the three of us, Weber had the best chance to keep his balance. He never had participated in any expedition before and many unfavorable details of our work, the unnecessary troubles which were the source of real torture for Kozhevnicov and me, were for Weber simply a few more incidents to be expected in such an expedition as ours.

Cape Shelagski was a large stock of granite almost completely worked out of slate. In many places it dropped to the sea in almost vertical cliffs about three hundred feet high. From the continental side, it was surrounded by low land, thus repeating features of both Baranov Capes of the Arctic shore. Its height of about twelve hundred feet corresponded closely to that of the Bolshoi Baranov Cape. Apparently this altitude was typical for the top of the mountains which we had seen near the shore on the previous part of our trip.

While my companions were moving on, I stayed at our camp on the Yanragaiveyam River to make arrangements with several Chukchi for winter travel by dog team. The great difficulty of dealing with Chukchi is a result of the lack of any social organization among them. They live in settlements of several *yerangas*, but no such settlement, however large, could be called a community, for each *yeranga* and the family it houses is an independent social unit. No settlement has a representative with whom it is possible to transact business. To organize a dog team, each dog owner must be dealt with separately. All other Siberian natives have administrative units—a village, a group of villages, or a tribe—and each unit has a representative to act for its members. The representative receives the money and distributes it among the hired people. He has authority among his people and is recognized by the government which appoints or approves him. Early attempts by Russian authorities to introduce such an institution among the Chukchi failed; when they appointed a Chukcha to act as an Elder or leader, he was considered as an official only by the Russians who appointed him. To his own people he was merely one of them, without authority or functions to perform. At the time of our expedition these attempts had been forgotten; even the collection of tribute from the Chukchi had been given up as hopeless. Apparently Russian authorities had decided to ignore the Chukchi or to treat them as an independent tribe. Consequently, in contrast to the ease with which the Yakutsk government could organize travel to the north through areas where natives had their own officials, the administration could deal with Chukchi only as we did, directly with the individual owner of dogs and reindeer.

Several Chukchi immediately offered me their dogs and personal help as drivers. On the first day I engaged five teams, but only to go as far as Cape North. The dogs had been underfed because of poor seal and walrus hunting that summer, and I could start my travel only after putting the dogs on a good diet. We killed several reindeer and, since the summer work had left our horses in such poor condition that it was hardly possible to return them to the Koluima River, they also were condemned to use as dog food. Still, I did not want to kill these animals until after we had moved as far east as possible, for rumor had it that hunting had been poor everywhere in the Arctic and that dogs were starving along the entire coast.

It took some time to find four more teams. Several Chukchi had dogs but could not decide to let us have them. Most of the owners were from Shelagski Cape and seemed to find it necessary to do all the bargaining there. Kuropachka, a Chukcha who hailed from the Koiveyan River, was quite ready to let us hire his dogs, but did not want to close the deal anywhere but there. I was not particularly disturbed by the delay because it would be at least three weeks before the sea near the shore would be frozen so that we could start. With every day my hope of using this time to push our baggage farther east and to locate a food cache there for our dogs grew less and less, and finally had to be abandoned. Summer was already over. Shortly after our arrival at the Yanragaiveyam camp, a strong northwestern wind pushed the floating ice toward the shore and the temperature dropped below freezing point. It snowed, and the snow remained on the ground. In Arctic and Subarctic regions spring and autumn are short, mere preludes to summer and winter. We knew that winter was close and that we had to keep this in mind while making new plans. Our reindeer were in bad shape and were needed for return travel of our Lamuts and the other people whom I did not expect to take along. Part of the deer I could push eastward, if only to slaughter them there for a food depot. Engaged in a complete reorganization of the expedition, I was unable to go myself and could not let my companions go. Kozhevnicov was already talking about the necessity of breaking up the expedition and turning back. I could not depend on Weber, as the trip was too severe a test for his inexperience, so I dropped the plan and to their great pleasure permitted the Lamuts to return home sooner than they had expected.

Following local customs, before our final separation from the Lamuts, I held a kind of festival with competitive games and prizes. Wrestling and racing were the most important events. Races went on for tremendous distances. Several miles were covered by the rivals who started from the camp, ran to a certain point, turned, and ran back to the camp. There a prize in the form of a brick of tea or a bundle of tobacco suspended on a pole was waiting for the champion, invariably a Lamut. The Chukchi were stronger but heavier than Lamuts, who were regular racers. Chukchi had first place in wrestling, and the Lamuts did not even compete in this field. In the women's race the prize was taken by our Ulyana, who came out far ahead of her Chukchi rivals.

Apparently the Chukchi did not like to be beaten by Lamuts all the time, and one young Chukcha did not run all the distance to the turning point before coming back. Naturally he came in first and won the prize. After a while the other runners came in with a Lamut in the lead and the cheating was discovered. I told the self-made champion to hand over the tea brick to the Lamut, but he looked very gloomy and apparently intended to keep the prize in spite of argument. Russian workmen tried to persuade me to drop the matter, to leave the prize with the Chukcha and give the Lamut another brick. "What is the value of a brick to us?" they argued. "A quarrel with the Chukchi will be very harmful now when we are dependent upon them." I had observed this fear of trouble with Chukchi more than once among the Russians from Koluima River. I told the Chukcha that I would disqualify him and not permit him to take part in any of the other games unless he gave the prize to the real winner. Chukchi are great sportsmen and the fear of such disqualification worked better than anything else. The Lamut got his prize and the incident was forgotten. The offender, I recall, was reconciled later by some other prize which he won in wrestling.

I had hoped to use the festival to get some information about the shore along which we expected to travel now, but found it extremely difficult to get any kind of information from Chukchi. Their knowledge of their country was limited to the area visited by themselves, and they had slight interest in anything lying beyond that area. Chukchi often surprised us by their low intelligence. For example, the Chukcha Kuropachka told me that in his youth he had visited the winter harbor of the *Vega*, the ship of the Nordenskiold Expedition which in 1878–1879 wintered near the Koliuchin Bay. When I told Kuropachka the name of the Chukcha whom Nordenskiold considered as head of local natives, there were no limits to his surprise. He immediately asked if I had been on that expedition also. I tried to explain to him that I had learned the name by reading about the expedition, but he and other Chukchi could not understand how anyone could get information about something he had not witnessed. We had the impression that some Chukchi considered writing as a kind of sorcery. After the episode concerning the Nordenskiold Expedition, Kuropachka told other Chukchi that a head of a Russian expedition may look like other people, be dressed in the same way, be capable of the same work as others, but that he had abilities distinguishing him from other people. But we could not get from the Chukchi any information of importance. Perhaps such low mentality is found only among the most western Maritime Chukchi staying near Shelagski Cape. They recognized their lower culture, at least in comparison with Chukchi living near Bering Strait, because they told us that the latter considered them to be wild animals.

The most important topic of conversation with the Chukchi was our future travel by dog team. When I mentioned my desire to learn about the driving of dogs, I was told that the Chukchi had deliberated upon our abilities as eventual drivers and had come to the conclusion that in this respect there could be no doubts about me! As they told Berejnov, they found me very "soft," which in the language of the Koluima Russians corresponds to being alert. Weber, who was a tall, well-built young man, they found too stiff for such work as dog driving, too unadaptable. Kozhevnicov was rejected because of his nervousness and irritable nature. Chukchi who keep themselves under perfect control did not approve of Kozhevnicov's sudden blushing. They commented upon the fact that his nose (which had once been frostbitten) was very susceptible to cold.

Our small holiday marked the complete reorganization of the expedition. From all our party I decided to take along only Berejnov and Rumyanzev. Kipriyanov, Shculev, and Yakut Mitrophan were sent back with our Lamuts, all three accepting their discharge with frank pleasure. Kipriyanov had a chance to save his face because he was given our mail and had in charge all our collections and some nonessential supplies which presented difficulties of transportation. Only Berejnov was willing to travel with us as far as necessary. When Rumyanzev learned of his appointment, he announced emphatically that he would not go eastward at all but instead would stay at Shelagski Cape and find some other means of returning to Koluima, since I did not permit him to use our reindeer. His desire to sever so quickly his connection with the expedition and his readiness to take the rather doubtful chance of finding immediate transportation at Shelagski Cape made me a little suspicious of his motives. He claimed that his reason for going home was to care for his family. He told me that his appointment to the expedition had happened so quickly that he had had no time to prepare his family for the coming winter. I needed a second man badly and told Rumyanzev that in leaving the expedition without my consent he was breaking the contract, with evil consequences for himself and his folk. I told him also what he already knew, that I could supply his family better and more quickly than he could by an order to the Koluima authorities. At last Rumyanzev yielded, and immediately a Chukcha friend, with whom in the past he had traded, also changed his mind. I knew that this Chukcha had a good dog team and could not understand his reasons for not wishing to rent the team to the expedition. After he learned that Rumyanzev was going with us, he offered me his team and services until we should reach the final point, Bering Strait. I rented another dog team from a Chukcha who had recently lost his father; in conformity with Chukchi mourning customs he might not travel for a year, so this dog team had no driver.

I rented one more dog team from Chukcha Kuropachka, whom I had surprised so much with my information about Nordenskiold's Expedition. Kuropachka could not go with us, because he was ready to move from the coast and follow his herd of reindeer, part of which had been near the sea during the past summer. Kuropachka was dependent on his reindeer for his livelihood, but since he did not have them in sufficient number he was forced also to use dogs for transportation. His poor relative was introduced to us, instructed to prepare everything needed, and to travel with us to Bering Strait.

To finish all our business with Kuropachka I had to journey to the Koiveyam River where he was staying for the summer. Kozhevnicov and Weber were located here very comfortably in our *chum*. Weber, who had lived here three weeks, was on friendly terms with the local people and had even begun to speak the Chukchi language. We killed our last horses at this time and made a cache of dog food. We became also the proud owners of our own dog team which was, however, not very much to be proud of. It had been collected dog by dog, and bartered from local Chukchi for anything which they wished to trade. Some of the dogs bought in this way were very old, others just-grown pups. We also had several bitches which are not considered good team dogs. Although our team was of a lower quality than average, it could carry a driver and about two hundred pounds of baggage. In case of an emergency we could perhaps save the better dogs by killing some of the poor ones for food. The dogs we bought cost us about the same as rented dogs or a little less, although with rented dogs we received a *narta*, harness for the whole team, and the services of a driver.

As staple payment for dogs we gave tea, tobacco, sugar, teakettles, skins of wolverines which I had brought for that purpose from Yakutsk, and skins of ice foxes for which I had bartered with Reindeer Chukchi during the past summer. To the Chukcha who could not travel with us because of his mourning, I promised to bring from Bering Straight a Winchester rifle with a box of ammunition. With the exception of this Winchester everything was paid for in advance. One Chukcha asked for a part of his payment in cash. He received a number of silver rubles, rolled them in his hands, and then tried to buy something from us in a quite funny way, offering one ruble for something which was at least ten times as expensive. After a few experiments of this kind which apparently did not please him at all, he returned all the money. Chukchi were extremely anxious to barter my Russian army rifle, although some American rifles in their hands were by no means poor weapons. Kuropachka became eager for a Colt forty-five automatic when he saw that one bullet could fell such a formidable animal as a horse. Disappointment was great when we refused to barter either the army rifle or the Colt automatic. To every owner of dogs I was forced to give, as a kind of premium, several bottles of vodka, but I made it a condition that he take it home and dispose of it there. I did not at all like this supplement to wages but could not avoid it. I am quite certain that without vodka it would have been impossible for us to rent even a half of the teams which we finally collected.

On October third I returned to Shelagski Cape where I was to collect all rented dog teams and where our travel eastward was to begin. Kozhevnicov and Weber waited for me at the Koiveyam River.

It was already winter and I left the place by dog team with a Chukcha on his *narta* as a passenger. It was my first experience driving dogs, even quite passive ones, and I was very anxious to observe everything of this new art. I did not know at that time that within a few days I should have need of mastery of the art. We drove along the shore and in many places over sea just frozen. In such cases my driver stopped the dogs and examined the ice with his knife. Everywhere the ice was thin, but it was strong enough for our light *narta* carrying two people and very little baggage. We crossed the largest surface of the newly frozen sea accidentally without any preliminary test. When we came to the sea, we stopped the dogs. The driver was just about to test the safety of the ice when suddenly our dogs sighted a wolverine on the opposite side of the frozen area and in no time at all we were off, with dogs barking, howling, and doing their best to reach the other side as soon as possible. It is rather difficult to brake a *narta* on smooth ice, and under the conditions of this ice it was dangerous, for it was thin enough to be broken through with the stick which is used as a brake. We had no choice on this mad run, we could only try not to be thrown off the *narta*. When we came to the shore we stopped for a moment while my driver cut the straps binding three dogs to the main strap. They ran after the wolverine and the Chukcha followed them with his Winchester, returning a few minutes later with the dead animal.

Berejnov waited for me at Shelagski Cape. Again we had difficulty getting the Chukchi to begin the trip. The sea was already frozen, as I had tested on my first dog trip, yet no Chukcha hired by us was ready to start. All of them told me they could not leave their families before they finished moving, repairing, and becoming reinstalled for winter in their *yerangas*. For this operation they needed windless days not very common at this time of year. Again I think that this obduracy had something to do with ritual, perhaps dating back to the time when Maritime Chukchi had reindeer and wandered after the fashion of their brothers still in possession of reindeer herds. Every fall the Maritime Chukchi wandered also, but literally for a distance of only a few hundred feet, as I had observed at Shelagski Cape.

Dwellings of Chukchi, Maritime and Nomadic alike, are constructed in the form of a huge hemispherical tent, made, in the typical case, of the chamois prepared from reindeer leather. In the east, chamois is often replaced with linen sail cloth of American origin. Such a tent, called a *yeranga*, is built very stoutly with a strong wooden frame inside and bound with leather straps outside. The latter often are tightened by suspending heavy stones from them. Owing to its strong structure and hemispherical form the *yeranga* resists heavy winds of the coast. I neither witnessed nor ever heard of any *yeranga* being blown over by a storm. Chukchi do not live in the *yeranga* itself but use it as a storehouse where more valuable objects are kept. Food sometimes is prepared in the *yeranga* and dogs find within a shelter when the weather is exceptionally bad.

For a dwelling, the people used the *polog*, or box-shaped tent made of reindeer skins, suspended within the *yeranga*. Its dimensions correspond to the size of the family, sometimes so closely that very little floor space remains unoccupied when the whole family retires, and Chukchi sleep on the floor in close proximity. It would be a hard job to handle the large and heavy *yeranga* cover during the windy day, and this fact was one of the reasons why the Chukchi were waiting for good weather to prepare their dwellings for winter. Besides that, it was necessary to patch the cover here and there, and this could be done only from the outside. When the Chukchi move they have no shelter throughout the long day, for other Chukchi of the settlement engage in the same business on the same day.

With Berejnov we did everything possible to hasten our start, but not until the twentieth of October were we able to leave Shelagski Cape. Observing our impatience, some of our future drivers did not miss the opportunity for extortion. They told me that they could not fix their *yerangas* for winter with the aid of their families only, so I had to hire helpers for them. All that time, in temperature below freezing, Berejnov and I lived in a tent which moisture as much as cold soon made uncomfortable. Walls and everything inside were covered with frost which every day thickened. I wished, however, to keep away from Chukchi as long as possible and to ask hospitality from them only when necessary.

14

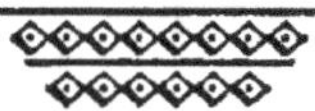

THE ART OF DOG DRIVING

ALMOST everybody knows something about dog driving in Alaska, Canada, Labrador, and other Arctic and Antarctic areas. Yet, outside of the region itself, very little is known about dog driving in northern Siberia, although in that country it is an old and original art. In many respects, however, it differs from dog driving anywhere else.

The Siberian dog sledge is called a *narta* and in its mechanical construction is similar to the *nartas* used north of Yakutsk. *Narta* runners are about ten feet long and bend upwards at the front ends. They bear four pairs of vertical supports on which are fixed, parallel to the runners, two long bars. The fore ends of the latter are bound together with the upper bent ends of the runners. Two side parts of a *narta*—runners, vertical supports, and longitudinal bars—are connected by means of horizontal crosspieces about two feet long running between the vertical supports at the middle and ends of the latter. Vertical supports and runners are fitted to each other by joints and bound with leather straps. The same joining of cross members connects the middle parts of the vertical supports to the opposite sides of the sledge. The upper frame is constructed more rigidly, although the longitudinal bars and upper horizontal cross members, as well as the connection of the whole frame with upper ends of vertical supports, are made with leather straps only. The fore ends of the longitudinal bars and runners of one side are connected with corresponding parts of the other side by means of a strong wooden bow bound with leather straps. No nails or any other metal parts making a permanent immobile connection are used in the construction of the *narta*, the whole strength of which lies in its elasticity.

In spite of the light build of a *narta* in general, it can stand a bad road where a sledge with more rigid construction would break into pieces; and if the *narta* should break, it is not difficult to repair. *Nartas* used by Russians and Chukchi are constructed in exactly the same way, the only difference being that Russian *nartas* are usually higher than those used by Chukchi. Chukchi *nartas*, therefore, are easier to manage, as they do not capsize as easily, but they have less clearance and do not pass over the uneven road as easily as the Russian variety.

Dogs are harnessed to the Siberian *narta* by means of a strong leather strap, usually made of walrus leather, with one end fixed to the front bow. Along this strap at certain distances from the bow are fixed small paired leather straps with small loops at their ends. Every dog has an individual harness running around the neck and body, ending in a short strap with a piece of wood fixed at its end. By means of these loops and pieces of wood, dogs are firmly and quickly connected in pairs with the main strap. There are no reins between the dogs and the driver, and the whole management of a team depends on the intelligence of the animals, or rather of the dog leader especially trained for this purpose and previously selected from among a number of dogs. The largest number of dogs in a Siberian team is fourteen. If dogs are well fed, but neither fat nor exhausted by previous work, a team of fourteen strong dogs can carry about one thousand pounds over good hard snow, maintaining an average speed of about ten miles per hour for a number of hours.

The steering of the Siberian *narta* differs from that of the American sledge because the sledges are not alike in construction. The Eskimo sledge, or its improved version, the American, has at its rear a back reaching above the waist of a driver. The driver stands on the ends of the runners with his hands on the upper edge of the back. Jumping from the runners and pushing or pulling from the rear of the sledge, he steers it very easily on the slippery road. The Siberian *narta* has a special steering bow fixed to the second vertical support across the sledge in such a way that the top of the bow is above the upper surface of the *narta* for about eighteen inches or two feet. A driver sits behind this bow with his feet hanging on the right side of the sledge or with the right foot on the runner; the left hand he keeps on the top of the bow.

To steer, the driver jumps off the sledge, pulls or pushes it by means of the vertical bow, and jumps up on his seat again. Steering is easier than in the American sledge because the effort is applied about at the middle of a sledge. Logically, from the position of the driver during travel, the Eskimo sledge has transportation for its purpose rather than speedy driving, whereas speedy driving is the goal of the Siberian *narta* driver. In both cases a passenger, if any, sits in almost the same part of a sledge, in front of the driver in the American sledge, behind him in the Siberian one. A Siberian driver, owing to his fore position, has a clearer view of the road than the American one, which is very important because runners must be directed at all times over the smooth snow or ice. Even a small piece of ice, wood, or stone protruding from the smooth ice is something to be avoided, especially when the speed is great. The excrements of a dozen or so dogs add to the troubles of a driver. If they are run over, the excrements freeze to the surface of the runners and increase resistance tremendously, so that quite often a driver must stop and clean the runners.

The *narta* upsets very easily and keeping it in balance is another job of a driver. I never had a chance to drive an American sledge but I am almost certain that preventing one from upsetting would be a much more difficult task than with a Siberian *narta*, because the American driver balances his sledge chiefly with the strength of his arms whereas the Siberian driver balances chiefly with the weight of his body. For example, when the road slopes toward the left, a driver in Siberia would stay on the right runner and balance his *narta* in that way. If the sloping is too great, the driver, with his left hand on the right side of the vertical bow and his feet on the right runner, thrusts his body as far from the *narta* as possible, often assuming an almost horizontal position. If the road slopes toward the right, the driver works on the left side of the *narta*. On an uneven road, going at great speed, a Siberian dog driver has a regular vaulting job.

The American dog sledge has a foot brake, which is undoubtedly a great improvement. In Siberia a *narta* is braked with a strong stick about three feet long which has an iron spike on one end. The stick is driven between the runners in front of the second vertical support when the *narta* is braked. The same stick is used to punish, in a very sensible way, a dog at fault. With faultless aim the driver throws the stick spear-wise at the culpable dog, always with the end opposite to that bearing an iron spike. The stick is picked up by the driver from the ground when the *narta* rushes by. As one may infer from this short description of managing a dog team, the driver has not very much opportunity to keep his seat. On a good road with good dogs and a load not very heavy for the dog team the driver works all the time. Heavy men not accustomed to physical exercise, or men with heart trouble or advanced in years, could not be dog drivers except on overloaded sledges. These were the matters which our workmen and Chukchi had considered very carefully when they pondered over our potentialities as eventual dog drivers!

Russians and, following their example, Chukchi, do everything possible to increase the gliding qualities of runners. A Russian proverb says: "Be ready with a cart in winter, with a sledge in summer." Dog drivers of northern Siberia follow that rule, at least its second part. The making of the most important part of sledges, the runners, begins a long time before their use. When possible, they are hewed out of a young birch tree and bent at the ends while the wood is still green. After the runners become well seasoned, they are shaped into their

final form and allowed to lie in a lake for the whole summer where they become well soaked with water. As I
saw during the preparation for my trip, runners are
sometimes taken out of the water from beneath ice. Such
runners are considered by Russians the best ones for the
coldest season. While traveling, every morning the driver
turns over his *narta* and wipes the runners with a piece
of fur soaked in lukewarm water, which forms a thin,
icy crust. This ice crust on the runners is usually renewed
in the middle of the day. When the sledge runs over dog
dung or other dirt, the runners must first be scraped with
a knife, and then again be coated with ice.

Apparently this method of preparing runners for better gliding was never known outside of Siberia and
never used by Arctic travelers. The frozen runners,
however, cannot be used in a comparatively warm
season, nor at the beginning of winter when the sea
ice is covered with slush or brine. Then the best runners
are those fashioned from long strips of whale jawbone,
which the Russians simply called "bones." During very
recent years American traders in the east have been im-
porting iron runners for dog sledges, which, through
many *intermediaire* owners, found their way not only to
the western natives but to the Russians on the Koluima
River as well, where they are called "iron bones." A good
example of how words lose their primary meaning! Russians find iron runners good for driving under average
conditions but not for use in very cold weather when,
according to their observations, iron sticks to the ice or
hard snow and does not glide as easily as iced wooden
runners.

15

LIFE IN A POLOG

WHEN we arrived at the Etonnik Settlement near Billings Cape we did not put up our *chum*, but stopped with Era, a Chukchi, crawling directly into his *polog*. Other teams stayed with other natives. Era at once pulled out his store of walrus meat, chopped it, and began to feed the dogs of his guests, following the local custom. Such hospitality is general, and every Chukcha coming to his friend for the night could be sure that he and his dogs would be treated well, and he was obligated to the same behavior when he became the host. In our case, of course, the natives expected payment for food and some-times even asked for something. I was certainly ready to give them anything, for their reception was such a relief to me that for the first time since the beginning of our dog travel I felt some assurance of eventual success.

Having become guests of Chukchi we naturally saw more of their intimate life than when we stayed in our *chum* or tents. As I have already mentioned, the Chukchi live in *pologs*, box-like tents made of reindeer skins and fixed within *yerangas*. Floors are usually made of seal skins. All walls of a *polog*, with the exception of the front wall, are stretched by means of wooden ribs and are immobile. The front wall is suspended free and functions as the door. To enter the *polog* it is necessary to lift the lower border of the front wall, crawl underneath, and drop the wall or curtain. Except for such entrances, a *polog* is closed completely without the slightest circulation of air. Only once did I see one with some kind of ventilation: at the back end was fixed the sleeve of a fur coat opening into the *yeranga* from which I distinctly saw smoke going out. Heat and light in a *polog* are given by lamps filled with blubber oil. Wicks are made of reindeer moss arranged along one border of the stone lamp to burn in a row of small bright flames. To repair these wicks and to equalize them so they do not smoke is a job in which the women attained great perfection. Since a *polog* is small and wonderfully insulated from outside cold, it is well heated by the lamps, the temperature inside rising very quickly to near ninety degrees.

Our first experience as guests in a *polog* was rather embarrassing and I cannot say I was very comfortable. Upon entering, a traveler immediately begins to undress himself. Native men naked to the waist, sweating, smelly, hunting for parasites, making water not only in the presence of women but with their assistance, was not so pleasant to see. All women are naked except for a narrow leather belt and, sometimes, a string of beads. The company of these women, some of them young, well-built, attractive, did not make us feel easy. There are certain conventional limits to this undressing, however: the women would be embarrassed without their belts, the men without their trousers. While changing their trousers the men always try not to expose themselves. Weber was criticized because sometimes while dressing or undressing he walked about the *polog* in only a shirt. I will never forget the embarrassment of a Chukcha to whom we gave a suspensory. He permitted us to show him how to put it on only after very noticeable hesitation, and his front was covered with large drops of sweat during the whole process.

Despite this evidence of modesty among Chukchi, there is great freedom between the sexes, and every girl has a right to dispose of herself as she likes, until she marries. Whether this freedom accounts for it or not, the men, even newcomers, ignore the women completely, and we noticed that the girls paid no attention to the men either, but went about as if they were alone in the *polog*. They did not try to attract our attention, although undoubtedly we were interesting people to them. When a girl is ready to give herself she does so from choice, not because she is sold or forced to do so. Days passed before we became accustomed to these conditions and, like the native men, we paid no attention to the naked women. As I observed their customs I said to myself, "The word 'coquette' is not in the vocabulary of these people." That is also true of other Siberian natives whom I have chanced to observe, but the thought is more impressive in a *polog* in close proximity to half-naked men and women than in the company of fully-clad people.

The freedom of sexual relations ends with marriage, however. Not only the husband, but also the wife feels the bondage of the marital tie. My impression was that marriages among natives are usually broken only by death, and only rarely by separation. Among the Chukchi there exists a custom relating to marriage that is not practiced by other Siberian natives. When a Chukcha visits a friend, the host offers his wife to his guest as a mark of hospitality. Often the host even goes to another *polog* to sleep in order that his friend may have complete freedom. When the host visits his former guest he expects the same favor and receives it. A Chukcha may offer his wife to a complete stranger if he is an honorable visitor. Refusal to accept this honor or to pay attention to the wife of the host is considered an insult. On the other hand, if the guest behaves as is expected of him, the next morning the husband may present him with a gift.

A traveler stopping at a *polog* gives his fur clothes to the women who dry and repair them. This precaution is particularly important for boots and gloves, because the danger of frostbite is greatly increased when footwear is not perfectly dry. For this reason everyone changes his outdoor boots for lighter ones as soon as he enters a *polog*. Warm heavy boots used during the travel would be soaked with perspiration if kept on in a warm *polog*, and would become a real danger the next day when used outdoors before being dried out. I once saw a traveling Chukcha with no baggage on his *narta* except for a pair of boots which he would put on at his night lodging.

The time of undressing and changing of boots is also used for destroying lice. That was, alas, our job every evening, for only by constant effort was it possible to keep the undesirable population of our bodies under a certain control. Chukchi eat the parasites, often offering them to each other. There is, however, a convention which limits the practice of that amenity to blood relatives!

All arms are left outside the *polog*. In the case of rifles, this is a custom dictated by the necessity of preventing them from rusting. I was told that when Chukchi procure vodka to drink in their *polog*, they first look very carefully to see that nobody carries a knife. I had my knife sewed to the right side of my trousers and in that way went into a *polog* armed. I noticed that my knife attracted attention and sometimes criticism.

The *polog* is the woman's realm. The men of the family are only guests within. They come inside in the evening, eat supper, stay for the night, and leave after breakfast. Even when men do not go anywhere they usually remain outdoors, doing some work around the house, or simply loafing. During the daytime, men go indoors only when the weather is stormy or to do work which cannot be done outside. Even boys are kicked out, and only the little ones remain with the women who have plenty of work to fill their entire day. Immediately after breakfast they clean the *polog* and air it somewhat. Among the Reindeer Chukchi the *polog*, loosely suspended within the *yeranga*, is taken off almost every morning, well beaten with sticks to clean the rime from it, and suspended again. Among Maritime Chukchi, the cleaning of the *polog* is done on the spot. The women allow no one to come into the *polog* with snow on his boots or clothes, and special sticks made of reindeer horns, always found near the entrance, are used for beating off snow. I remember one day we were traveling through a heavy snow storm, and not only were my clothes packed full of snow, but even my beard was transformed into a block of snow and ice. A woman cleaned my face carefully before she permitted me to enter.

Food when cooked, which is seldom, is prepared over a fire in the *yeranga*. In most cases food, almost exclusively meat and seldom fish, is served in rough form, often frozen; it is usually chopped and seasoned with blubber oil. We ate seal, walrus, reindeer meats, and such select tidbits as the skin of a whale or fins of walrus. Fish served frozen in north Siberian fashion in my opinion makes quite a palatable meal. Weber, however, could neither appreciate it at all nor even distinguish it from other frozen meats. He told us many times that to him it tasted no different from crushed ice. Often the meat served was in such poor condition that we could not touch it, although our hosts did not pay any attention to the putrid smell.

Sometimes we prepared our own meals, using the Swedish kerosene stove which is well known in Europe under its trade name Primus. Unfortunately the Primus made some noise, which made it objectionable to the Chukchi, not as a noise but as a possible source of evil. Once, in a *polog* where we had used the Primus, when a little boy became sick his parents were ready to look for the source of his sickness in our machine. Upon his recovery the next day, however, our noisy machine was forgiven.

The lamps which are used for light and heat are also used for making tea. Making tea is always a long process because of the necessity of first melting ice or snow. Stored water seldom is available, for in most cases the water is used for drinking before all the ice is melted. Chukchi do not wait to make tea in boiled water but put in crushed brick tea when the water is, in their opinion, hot enough. When some of the tea is drunk, water (usually ice-water) is added to the teakettle still hanging above the fire. Tea prepared in that way is very little like the drink made of the same tea but in the proper way, hence we always preferred to make our own tea on the Primus. When we had tea we shared with all the occupants of the *polog* our sugar and dried bread, both products very rare and highly appreciated.

Fire is extremely important in the primitive life of natives and for that reason its use is always surrounded with special customs or superstitions. I have already mentioned the objections against our Primus; another objection is to fire brought from someone else's home. It is also objectionable to use strange kettles. Matches are used by Chukchi, but on certain occasions the fire has to be started in the old-fashioned way by rubbing together two pieces of wood.

We provoked some criticism by our night excursions from the *polog* after we were installed there for the night. Every night we had observations to make outdoors and when the work was astronomy we were busy late into the night. The oil lamps were kept burning, and with our repeated going out and coming back, talking, and so on, we were certainly an annoyance to the people already sleeping. Chukchi once settled for the night went out only in the case of extreme emergency. It was not only the natural lack of inclination to get up, to put on clothes and take them off again, but there was a superstition that night was full of evil forces which could not penetrate into the *polog* unless it was opened. Physiological emergencies that sent us out did not trouble the Chukchi at all. From time to time one would say a few words to the woman nearest him and she would give him a ladle and carry it away full. The urine was poured into some kind of bucket and used for washing dishes and hands. We were very careful to have our dishes cleaned before the women started their work, but sometimes we were not quick enough and our dishes, spoons, cups, and forks passed through the native kind of cleaning. At such times we were comforted by the fact that we also used the serving dishes of our hostess, which passed through such a washing several times every day. Sometimes when a woman found that she had not enough stored urine for her work, she stopped for a while, sat down, produced the necessary liquid, and continued her work.

Arriving at a settlement, members of our party always tried to find quarters with different families, as it was practically impossible for all of us to be housed in one *polog*. We three and our two interpreters sleeping together usually filled a *polog* to capacity, insofar as the area of the floor and volume of air were concerned. I remember one really terrible night at the Kenmankautir Settlement, near Yacan Cape. In a *polog* about twenty feet long, nine wide, and not quite seven high, eighteen people were sleeping. There was no ventilation. Several oil lamps were burning all evening and the greater part of the night because we expected to make an astronomical observation. In no way could Weber adjust his lanterns to burn brightly enough and I was no more successful. Suddenly the true explanation of the trouble flashed through my mind. I advised Weber to start the observation at once and not to worry any more about lanterns. Outside a few minutes later the lanterns burned brightly —there simply had not been enough oxygen for the flame inside! I was not surprised, therefore, later on when my stearine candle flickered so much I could hardly write my notes and letters to be sent with Kozhevnicov.

The worst part of that particular *polog* was that its inhabitants were infected with scabies, and avoided even by other Chukchi. Unfortunately, we did not know it before we entered and once there could not achieve any isolation. My neighbor on the floor, an old woman, scratched her body all the time, as did everybody else in the *polog*, with the exception of us newcomers. Looking at me for sympathy and comfort, she murmured all the time *etki-etki* (it is bad, it is bad). After all my work was done and I crawled into my bed, I could not sleep for the noise of scratching that came from all corners of the *polog*. Although I stayed for the night at the same place on my return trip without suffering any bad effects, Kozhevnicov was so infected that not until he reached Koluima could he get rid of the itch which he contracted there.

Chukchi, in common with all primitive people, are very fond of children. In the infected *polog* there was a five- or six-year-old boy blind from birth. Under the living conditions of Chukchi such a boy could be only a burden and I should not have been surprised had they disposed of him as they did their old or incurably sick people. I do not know the final fate of this boy but at that time he was everyone's pet. Women gave him the best pieces of food, and men invariably tickled his genitals when he passed nearby, in northern Siberia a very common way of caressing little boys.

At the Etonnik Settlement we had a very interesting incident. When we were ready to leave, a young Chukcha, the driver of Kozhevnicov's *narta*, told us that by no means would he travel further. After some questioning he explained that on that particular day we should pass a settlement where lived a Chukcha of whom he was afraid. Several years ago he had borrowed something from this Chukcha, and had not yet paid it back. He thought that the Chukcha would kill him. I told him that as long as he was employed by me nobody would dare touch him, at the same time granting Kozhevnicov permission to use arms if necessary. Kozhevnicov showed the driver his rifle and automatic and the Chukcha decided to take the chance, but not without some preparations on his own part. Shortly before starting he borrowed a Winchester from a friend. Since we traveled separately I had no idea what was happening to Kozhevnicov's driver or to Kozhevnicov himself and did not feel quite at ease. At the night camp I met both of them. The Chukcha had decided to jump directly into the lion's den and had led Kozhevnicov to his enemy's *yeranga*. There they partook of tea and left without any reference to the old debts. About three months later on my return travel I met the Chukcha who had frightened our driver so

much, and asked him if it was true that he had intended
to kill his debtor. He answered in the affirmative, and said
that he had changed his mind because he did not think
he might do anything against a man temporarily employed by me.

This case, together with some other small incidents
and information conveyed by our interpreters, showed
me that the natives living around Shelagski Cape were
not on friendly terms with far-eastern Chukchi. From my
own experience I could not look with favor upon the
Chukchi of Shelagski Cape. Sometimes they were arro-
gant, inclined to extortion, childish in handling their
business. Some of our drivers were even thievish, something rare among natives. A part of our dried bread, a
very important item indeed, was stolen. However, it was
more than possible that this was not a regular larceny
either. The driver in care of that supply occasionally
tasted this dainty stuff during the trip and consumed
more of it than he intended. I do not like to attribute
these negative characteristics to the Chukchi's contact
with Russian traders and members of local administration, but apparently I must. The higher cultural level of
eastern Chukchi can undoubtedly be attributed to their
contact with American traders. It should not be inter-
preted that I consider American traders as people of a
higher moral standard than the Russians, but in handling
business and in their behavior to the natives, the Americans were entirely different from the Russians. And again
I should not be misunderstood. These differences were
not national characteristics but depended rather on his-

torical, geographical, and economic conditions which were entirely different for the Americans near Bering Strait than for Russians on the Koluima River.

Although a Russian myself, I was a stranger in north-eastern Siberia, yet I could understand the psychology of Russians in dealing with the natives. Russians, beginning with the Zasyedatel Melnicov and ending with our workers, disagreed with me more than once in regard to my always kind, but straight and independent dealing with Chukchi, and frequently were even a little alarmed at possible consequences. I had, however, no reason to be sorry about the line of conduct taken. The natives learned very soon that my No meant *No* and my Yes, *Yes*, that I was rather generous in my payments, but at the same time stayed very closely to the conditions of any contract once it was made. I respected their customs and, while taking advantage of the hospitality of Chukchi, I tried to adapt to their living conditions as much as possible without attempting to become one of them. They repaid me with a certain respect, and forgave me such small violations of their customs as using our Primus in the *polog* and going in and out during the night. They appreciated the fact that I partook of their food without grimacing and that I disposed of it, hard and soft parts alike, just as quickly and efficiently as they did. They saw also that I could do everything that they or my workers could do and remain at the same time chief of the expedition!

My authority, once established and recognized, helped us a great deal. Only with some certainty of authority would I have risked as I did the punishing of the dishonest contractor Kuropachka with confiscation of his dogs, or insisted that the Chukcha driver who was afraid of his creditor should travel through the settlement in which the latter lived. My authority was perhaps less important with Chukchi in settlements through which we traveled than with our dog owners from the Shelagski Cape. Our meetings with the former were short, often not more than a night. Only a snow storm or our work ever kept us a whole day or more at any point. Native hospitality was always well paid for and usually we parted from the host with mutual regard.

Since we were staying nights exclusively with Chukchi, we traveled as they did from one settlement to another, provided that the distance between was about twenty miles, for that was the average distance we could survey during the short autumn days. Sometimes settlements were nearer to each other and we passed a *yeranga* where our drivers wished to stop with their friends, but we drove past. Sometimes it happened that distances between two settlements were considerably greater than twenty miles and we could not be through with our work in one day. There was nothing else to do in such cases but to go ahead to the settlement, make a stop there for a day and give Weber a chance to go back and finish the previous day's work. Our drivers did not like such retracing of a route already traveled over. Chukchi always leave their night camp considerably before dawn, and stop for the night before darkness. We left as soon as we had enough light for surveying and often reached the next settlement after dark.

Another source of misunderstanding was the impossibility of our planning the trip for the day to come, because we could not get from our drivers any reliable data about distances between different settlements. Yakuts or Tangus have the so-called *kess* for measuring road distances, a rather vague unit between four and five miles, but if Chukchi have any idea of measurement of distance we could not find it. We tried to get an idea about the distance ahead of us by comparison with others already passed. This ruse worked more or less satisfactorily when the distances were almost equal, but that was seldom the case. After a few bad experiences, the Chukchi's expression *"Kitt-kitt-warkin,"* that is, "a little greater," became for us more a source of fun than of information.

If Chukchi in general lacked the geographical abilities of the other northern natives, they nevertheless did possess a highly developed sense of orientation. I remember one day when we traveled through a terrible blizzard. Neither the direction of wind, which was irregular and constantly veering, nor the character of shore gave me any means of orientation. To make matters worse, the Chukchi cut across the low swamp and lake land reduced to uniformity by the snow cover. I was obsessed by a sense of going on and on blindly and breathlessly without ever being sure that we were not hopelessly lost, but we arrived at our next night camp without making any loops, a fact checked later through comparison with our survey.

Our Chukchi also disliked Weber's traveling along the line of the shore over a course that never permitted them to take short cuts. Sometimes, for reasons inexplicable to them, when the weather was good and the

Chukchi were in the mood to leave for the next camp immediately, we camped. Drivers were displeased also with a particular kind of competition which we made with dogs belonging to the expedition. According to local custom a dog traveler was permitted to leave along his route a completely exhausted dog and take a fresh substitute. On his way back the traveler would exchange dogs once more and reclaim his own rested animal. Such an exchange was considered a friendly service of a mutually beneficial character and was always performed without pay. But the reciprocity enjoyed by native drivers was lacking in our case and we had to pay for every dog exchanged. The number of dogs available for such an exchange was always limited and in some settlements we could not find any substitutes, but wherever extra dogs were present we managed first to exchange dogs from our own team, and drivers of the other teams resented this.

In a very naïve way the drivers asked me once to give them some barter material to pay for dog food. Since we paid for all food I answered naturally in the negative. After that they tried to make a new contract for the return trip from Bering Strait for no other purpose than to get some of our goods into their hands, and as at Cape Shelagski, they demanded everything in advance. To give the drivers a part of our supplies would mean to let slip from our hands the monopoly which made us masters of the situation and permitted our working when and how we pleased. So I answered the drivers that I found all these talks premature and that at Bering Strait we would have plenty of time for bargaining. Great was their disappointment and displeasure, but our Chukchi could not do anything. Small but often repeated events gradually spoiled our relations and at last brought a break, although fortunately not until the final point of our travel eastward at Dezhnev Cape on Bering Strait.

During the travel itself the Chukchi's discontent sometimes found expression in childish outbursts. I remember one morning I was dressing in the *polog* when Rumyanzev crawled in very excited and told me that Lubcha, the driver who had stolen or eaten our dried bread, had thrown from his *narta* two boxes and announced that he would not carry them any further. "All right," said I, "I shall look into it as soon as I am through putting on my boots." A few moments later I was outside but I did not find either Lubcha or the boxes which were so objectionable to him. When Rumyanzev told him that I should come out soon, Lubcha had immediately loaded the boxes on his *narta* and driven away in a hurry. I did not find him until that night's lodging, but did not mention anything about the morning incident.

Our drivers had told other Chukchi that they would not travel into the Koliuchin Bay region as we had planned at the beginning. I had learned of this murmuring from my interpreters before the Chukchi themselves had a chance to tell me about it. An opportunity for exploration of that practically unknown bay appealed to me very much. I saw, however, that the achievement of of that goal would not justify any additional discomfort or risk. The days were already very short, and the weather unstable. At least two weeks were necessary for this trip. There was no population along the bay shore, and for our camping and for feeding the dogs we must depend solely on our own supplies. Because of the poor seal hunting, it was impossible to expect to find such supplies at the coast. I knew also that under the present conditions it would be impossible for me to get our Chukchi to follow the provisions of our contract, and I did not like to lose face, never a good thing among natives. I decided, therefore, to leave the task of the exploration of the Koliuchin Bay to some traveler who might work there in more favorable circumstances than ours. At North Cape I left our *chum* which we had carried solely to make the journey to Koliuchin Bay. Shortly afterwards I informed our Chukchi that I was not expecting to travel into the bay region on account of the very late season.

From North Cape I sent back with Kozhevnicov two *nartas* of such dogs as were already quite exhausted. Partly for that reason and also because both his *nartas* were heavily loaded, chiefly with ethnographical collections which he had managed to collect during our sledge travel, Kozhevnicov's travel was very slow and difficult. He made only short trips by day, walking the greater part of the route. He was also handicapped by frequent blizzards, as was also the expedition in its movement eastward. The last two months of a year at the sea coast were always marked by unsettled weather. We separated at North Cape on the ninth of November.

Leaving us was very painful for Kozhevnicov and would have been avoided, if we had had better means of transportation. With Kozhevnicov we sent our last mail and different orders referring to our return road. I already had sent orders with Shculev and Kipriyanov for dogs which were to wait for us at Shelagski Cape. With Kozhevnicov's turning back I asked him to send dogs from Shelagski Cape as far eastward as North Cape.

Between Cape Kekurni and North Cape we traveled along a shore rather monotonous in appearance. Such capes as Billings and Yacan, although well expressed in the trend of the shore line, were just as high as the shores near by and "not conspicuous," to quote the characteristics given them by marine pilots. The inland mountains in their northern section were composed of rather low, inconspicuous hills, and only the mountains further south reminded one of those in the western part of our route. Shores in many places were rocky but often covered in part with snow. My geological observations unavoidably lost their continuity. This interruption was particularly annoying, because the geology of this part of the shore was apparently somewhat different from that which I had observed before, and I suspected the appearance of new geological formations here.

Areas between capes were occupied with large lagoons stretched along the shore for many miles and separated from the sea with low gravel banks. For hours and hours we drove along these banks. After this monotonous landscape North Cape, which was neither large nor high but conspicuous and well separated from the lowland around it, looked particularly picturesque. The Cape was composed of two parts which, from a distance, appeared to be two small round-topped islands. Since they had had no names I christened them in honor of my two companions. The western cape I called Utes Kozhevnicova (Kozhevnicov's Rock), the eastern one Utes Webera (Weber's Rock).

16

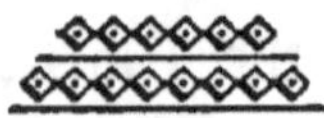

ᗞezhneᏉ cape

IN SPITE of the short periods of daylight Weber was able to survey over twenty-five miles daily. There was no more trouble with dog food because we now had fewer dogs, the settlements were more numerous, and the natives more prosperous. Our daily trips were about as long as those averaged by the Chukchi themselves. The only handicaps were blizzards, which kept us inside the *polog*. We dropped the survey of the very large lagoons, abundant along the eastern part of the shore, not only because we were short of time, but because we could not satisfactorily survey lagoons when winter conditions hid their low shores.

The coast southeast of North Cape was similar to that which we had passed northwest of the Cape. Outcrops of rocks were few and low. These features of the shore helped the progress of our travel, but not the study of geology. Cape Onman, at the entrance into Koluichin Bay, on the western shore of the latter, reminded us again of the capes on the Arctic shore between the Koluima River and Cape Shelagski. This Cape was more than twelve hundred feet high, with rocky cliffs dropping abruptly into the sea. Almost eight hundred feet high was Koluichin Island, a granite rock in the entrance to Koluichin Bay. We stayed on the island for a night, and the next day traveled to the eastern shore of the bay. The coast between Koluichin Bay and Cape Serdze-Kamen was similar to the shore northwest of the bay, as it also was low and abounded in lagoons with a few low rocky outcrops.

During this part of our travel I was rather surprised to observe an example of the Chukchi's indifference toward natural phenomena. The end of 1909 was noted for the appearance of a large comet. One clear evening the comet shone in all its beauty not very high above the horizon, and I expected to hear some questions from our drivers. Although they saw the comet, there was no talk about it among the Chukchi with whom we stayed for the night.

At the Onman settleme   we met a boy who carved ivory. Some of his work was done purely for sale to American traders and had no artistic interest, but a few small human figures, often in very peculiar poses, were remarkably well done, even though the only instrument .ich the young artist had was a small knife.

On November twenty-fourth we arrived at Serdze-Kamen Cape, where we stayed more than four days, waiting for the eclipse of the moon on November twenty-seventh, the observation of which was very important for us. The Russian name of this Cape means "a heart rock," and there is an allusion in Russian literature to the heart shape of the cape. Actually, however, the most ardent imagination could not discern such a shape.

The name originally was introduced in the sense of a core, referring to the northern end of the central ridge piercing the peninsula. The southern end of the same ridge on the northern shore of Anadyr Bay was also called Serdze-Kamen Cape on old Russian maps, but that name is not to be found on the more recent ones.

At the settlement on Serdze-Kamen Cape we met the first American seen by the expedition, a prospector named Wall, about whom I had been told back in St. Petersburg, the man whose schooner had been demolished by Chukchi. He had traded for a while near Bering Strait, and also was interested in gold mining.

When we met Wall, he was a man of middle age, staying at the settlement probably because he had no means of moving away. He was living with a Chukchi girl in the *yeranga* of his father-in-law, a rich Chukcha who seemed to be proud of having an American for a son-in-law. Psychologically the illiterate native and the highest government official of eastern Siberia were much alike! The Chukchi also liked Wall because he was very eager to hunt seals and never was too tired to go hunting. The American-Chukchi couple lived in their own *polog*, which we shared. Wall did not know what the word geologist meant and spent a long time looking for it in a small dictionary. The presence of a dictionary, a few numbers of the Alaska-Yukon Magazine, and a small phonograph, indicated that we were approaching a cultured people, although the *polog* with oil lamps, the almost nude young woman, and half-nude men were typical of Chukchi life.

Wall was the first man with whom I could converse without the assistance of interpreters. Among the

Chukchi we also found several men who knew a few English words and one or two who could even speak English at some length. Such had not been the case with the natives near the Koluima River, who spoke no Russian, but perhaps the reason was that Russians coming in contact with natives were more eager to learn their language than to teach them Russian.

We left Wall's *polog* on November twenty-eighth. In spite of the advanced time of year, the sea near Cape Serdze-Kamen was not yet completely frozen. Earlier, from the top of Onman Cape I had seen a large *polynia*, the end of which I could not distinguish, but we found enough ice for shore travel. In many places from Serdze-Kamen Cape the coastal mountains plunge toward the sea as high cliffs. The shore line could there be examined and surveyed only by boat or sledge travel on ice near the shore. On account of the open sea here and there along the shore, we journeyed over the mountains almost all the time and descended to the sea only at those places where we expected to stay for the night. All settlements in this part of the rocky coast, stretching for about forty-five miles, are located in the lower part of the narrow valleys. Traveling through the valleys we found, in several protected places, a few low shrubs of Alnus and Betula still in very poor shape, although we were already south of the Arctic Circle. After the endless tundras on which we had traveled during the whole summer we greeted these poor messengers of forests with great pleasure. The wide distances separating the settlements, the unfavorable weather, and our inability to follow the shore line as closely as was necessary prompted me to stop our survey at Serdze-Kamen Cape. For the section of the shore between that point and the Dezhnev Cape we had a survey made by the Russian Navy boat *Rasboinik* in 1884. For some reason, however, the Rasboinik Expedition had not made any astronomical observations. We determined astronomically the geographical position of Serdze-Kamen Cape and later of Dezhnev Post and Ugelen, thereby improving the *Rasboinik's* survey for cartographical purposes.

Traveling over a mountainous road much used by local people and covered therefore with hard snow, my driving abilities were again severely tested. I had to help the dogs up hill and pull against them on the way down. Because of the down-hill speed I had difficulty staying on my *narta*, which sometimes flew rather than slid. It was necessary to steer it, to maintain its equilibrium, and to use the brake constantly. More than once it upset. A split *narta* stops the dogs at once, and such an accident is not serious except for the loss of time and the extra, often heavy, work involved in righting it. Padded with warm thick clothes and hardened by travel, one can be thrown from one's *narta* without harm, even while driving at high speed. Once driving down the hill along the slope toward my left, with my left hand on the middle bow, feet on the right runner, and body hung out to balance the *narta*, suddenly I saw that the rear dog had collapsed and the next moment would be crushed. I jumped on the sledge, but before I could do anything in the way of braking, the *narta* overturned and threw me into the air. I landed on my head on the other side of the road and distinctly heard something crack in my neck, but felt no pain then or later.

After crossing a ridge, I arrived at the bottom of a hill almost exhausted, but always with a pride of achievement and a feeling that the exercises were becoming easier for me every day. What had begun as hard work was becoming good sport.

On the second of December we arrived at the Ugelen settlement located on the western side of Dezhnev Cape along the Arctic seashore, on the low bank separating a large lagoon from the ocean. The low shore was beyond the rocky coast of Serdze-Kamen Cape, more than twenty miles northwest of Ugelen. We passed this part of our travel very quickly, particularly because we made no survey here. Our road to the Dezhnev post followed the lowland bordering Dezhnev Cape from the west. This cape was quite similar to Shelagski Cape, but was larger, with an altitude close to three thousand feet, higher than the capes of the western part of the coast.

At our approach to Ugelen the Chukchi quite unexpectedly hoisted on a mast the Russian national flag. The colors stirred me; I was moved by such a display. My first intention was to take out my automatic and discharge a magazine as a salute, but I refrained, perhaps for the best. At that time the natives and Russians at the Dezhnev post were still not quite certain whether we were a scientific expedition or political fugitives from Turukhansk.

Besides the flag greeting, we also enjoyed a small reception at the most prosperous *yeranga*—a tea party in the large but now overcrowded *polog*. Our host belonged to the class of trading Chukchi which had appeared on the part of the coast visited by American traders. All the natives carried on trade occasionally, but Chukchi such as our host had accumulated some stores and even had small storehouses built outside the *yerangas*, where trade could be carried on with profit even in winter and spring. From such a trader I bought, for example, a brand new Winchester rifle and a box of ammunition which I had promised to bring to Shelagski Cape as payment for one dog team. Besides different new paraphernalia in the homes, such as talking machines with really impossible selections of records, the nearness to America was evident in the sailcloth covering on a few *yerangas* and in the use of whaleboats along with common leather *baidaras*. The hospitality offered us was not without a little material interest, as our host expected to receive something good to drink. My supply of alcohol by that time was exhausted, but I was so pleased with the whole reception and with the achievement of our goal, which had appeared almost impossible two months ago, that I promised to give our host the desired drink if he would go with us to Dezhnev Cape, our destination for the evening.

At the Dezhnev post we found a Russian colony of five people. The local chief of police, Captain Kalinnicov, was not there, and his duties were in the hands of Marchenco, an agent of a well-known Siberian firm whose factory had been established at the uppermost northeastern promontory of Asia.

The store in Marchenco's care hardly could be called

successful. Certainly the trouble lay with the natives, who had traded with Americans and who were for many years accustomed to commerce that essentially was seasonal and wholesale. At Marchenco's a native might go to the open shop anytime and buy commodities at retail prices. As everywhere, there was much window shopping, or perhaps it is better to say, shelf shopping. Chiefly because the natives were unable to estimate the value of what they wanted to buy or unable to give anything in barter, the trade was not without comedy, especially as the storekeeper had few visitors and a whole day at his disposal. For example, a Chukcha might want a teakettle in exchange for some item he had brought along. In Marchenco's opinion the teakettle was too valuable—a cake of soap would be about right. The Chukcha would take the soap, examine it with all five senses, and give it back. He understood only that the teakettle was not available to him, and for soap he had no use. So he began to look for something else among the assorted merchandise on the shelves of the store. Sometimes, however, grave tragedy was concealed in such an incident. Once Marchenco was trading in his usual jocular way with an old native woman who wished to have some cotton cloth for a new dress. His jokes, however, stopped at once when he learned that the woman was making preparation for her coming strangulation by her younger relatives. The killing of old people was practiced by the Chukchi not only when the victims were weak or incurably ill, but often merely because their younger relatives wanted them out of the way. A son who wanted to be the head of his father's house would limit his father's influence to some special small jobs and the father was compelled to follow the routine his son set up or risk his life. If in self-defense the father tried to eliminate the son, it would be in violation of a very old custom. Women were subject to the same treatment as men and were disposed of as often. The killer was usually a close relative and of the same sex as the victim. The old people accepted their coming destruction as unavoidable and did nothing either to retard or hasten it, but died when the moment came, always with great dignity.

Russian authorities did not try to prevent the killing of old people. Distances between the authorities and the killers were too great, and no information could ever be obtained from the Chukchi about such events. Among no other Siberian natives does this terrible custom exist.

Bettack, a German doctor, and Marchenco met us very cordially outside their home as we alighted from our *nartas*. As I learned much later in St. Petersburg, they had no idea whether we were scientists or political fugitives. When I addressed a remark to Weber in German, Dr. Bettack heard and understood us. He took Marchenco aside and whispered to him in a great excitement: "No, no, it was all wrong, this is a true expedition." In spite of that, five Chukchi with ready Winchesters sat awake all night in the *yeranga* of the American prospector, Carpenter.

We did not notice anything wrong, being quite excited with the well-built houses and the warm rooms lighted by strong kerosene lamps. We felt fine, seated on chairs before tables. Nor was it necessary to take off our clothes and kill the lice, the general battle with which we postponed until the next morning. We breathed regular air, not a mixture of air, oil smoke, and the odors of dirty, sweaty, naked bodies, and urine. News from Russia was several months old but still news to us. There was a phonograph, and records of good musical and vocal numbers. All of this was perhaps second- or third-rate comfort, but after three months of living in *pologs*, Bettack-Marchenco's dwelling seemed like a real palace. Next morning we bathed with plenty of soap and rubbing, shaved, had hair cuts, and became again our more or less civilized selves.

We stayed with our new Russian friends more than two weeks. The weather was very unstable; there were blizzards almost every day. We had hardly any days suitable for geological investigation of the area near the settlement, or clear nights for astronomical observations. Because of bad weather I was unable to visit the Eskimo settlement on Dezhnev Cape.

We met and became good friends with Carpenter, whose *yeranga* had been an ambush on the night of our arrival. Like Wall, he had a Chukchi girl for a wife and lived like a native in his own *yeranga*. We had, however, the impression that unlike Wall, he felt a little embarrassed about living in that fashion. At least, Carpenter never invited us into his *polog*, but always spoke with us in the *yeranga* or outside of it. Sometimes he gave the impression of being a rather intelligent man, at least not like the rank and file of prospectors. Other times we did not know what to think about him. He told Weber that once he stayed awake all night because he could not find out how much half of a quarter would be!

As for their homes, neither Carpenter nor Wall could change their native mode of life. The construction of even a small shack would cost more than a good *yeranga* and *polog,* and the difference in upkeep was still greater. A ton of coal at that time cost thirty dollars. The oil heat and light of *pologs* came as a by-product of hunting. Perhaps from the hygienic point of view *pologs* were even better adapted to local climatic conditions than other types of houses. During our travel and the time spent in *pologs* I never had any trouble with my health, but I contracted a bad cold shortly after our arrival at the Dezhnev post. It was very difficult to prevent draughts in rooms heated by iron stoves. My cold passed very quickly, however, and was less serious than Weber's illness. One morning when he came out to breakfast, I looked at him and said: "You eat too much here, my dear boy, you are becoming fat." With some irritation he answered that people who had not seen him for a long time would be better judges of his stoutness or thinness. Dr. Bettack looked at him also and said: "All that is quite right, but after breakfast come into my study; I should like to examine you." He did and found nephritis, which, fortunately, healed quickly with proper medical treatment.

Once more we had trouble with dogs. I expected to have our Chukchi from Shelagski Cape for our journey back. According to my information, western Chukchi after a travel like ours usually stayed on Dezhnev Cape for about a month and then started on the return trip, but this time they left the day after our arrival, without even renewing the talk of a new contract. One of the Chukchi had promised me in the very beginning to be available for us on the way back, but even that fellow abandoned me. I was told later that all the local natives were making fun of our former drivers for traveling home from the abundance of Dezhnev Cape with no merchandise on empty *nartas*. Such a thing was absolutely senseless to the practical-minded Chukchi, nor could our drivers explain their motives for such strange behavior. Probably local natives had an idea that it was I who was responsible for the whole matter, and were very anxious to find out what had happened among us. When I was again at Shelagski Cape, our former drivers offered their hospitality in a quite friendly way. Their sudden departure from Dezhnev Cape was probably on an inexplicable impulse, common enough among the Chukchi. I am almost certain that if they had been forced to remain for a few days, they would have forgotten their caprice and behaved like good children again. Unfortunately for me, I had to take advantage of the good weather during the first days after our arrival by beginning the old job of collecting dogs for the return travel.

We had three *nartas*: one previously rented, another with rather poor dogs collected in various places, and the third confiscated from Kuropachka. At the Dezhnev post I bought two strong young dogs for ten dollars each. They were the best looking animals, not only in my team but among all the dogs, with their only defect their youthfulness. They were only two years old and sometimes, when the work was not hard, they began to play with one another or with the other dogs.

Among the natives in our neighborhood we could not find any dogs, although I sent requests in different directions. When the blizzards came all communications were broken and several days passed before we were able to hire four-dog teams from Chukchi who were willing to help us as far westward as the North Cape.

17

TO SHELAGSKI CAPE AND SUKHARNOYE

WE LEFT our new friends and started westward on the nineteenth of December. The time was not favorable for traveling; it was the heart of winter, with the days at their shortest and the season at its coldest. We had no accurate record of the temperature because our alcohol thermometers were broken and mercury thermometers were not only useless at very low temperatures, but some of ours were graduated not very much below zero. I do not think, however, that the temperature dropped much below forty degrees, for I never heard the noise of breath which, according to my observations, appears when temperatures are running fifty below. My work as a driver kept me from being cold, and during all the trip I never once put on the heavy fur coat which I had on my *narta*. This fur coat, however, served me well when I traveled later as a passenger to Sredne-Koluimsk, Yakutsk, and Irkutsk.

We had no more work to do and could follow all native customs of travel. We broke camp long before dawn, drove over the usual road, and arrived at a new stopping place before darkness. The weather was good, the storms few and of short duration. I realized also that everywhere we had left behind a good impression; the natives greeted us as their old friends.

On the sixth of January, 1910, we arrived at North Cape. To our great and unpleasant surprise we did not find the dogs which Kozhevnicov was to have sent from Shelagski Cape. I thought that they might be late and waited three days, but Chukchi who arrived from the west during those days did not bring us any news. I had no doubt that the dogs had been sent from Koluima River to Shelagski Cape and, since there had been ample time for the animals to be sent on to us at North Cape, I was afraid that something had prevented Kozhevnicov from reaching the Cape. In this case the dogs would wait for us there, according to my first order.

I could not wait passively at North Cape any longer. I felt also that our three teams and the dogs of those Chukchi who had brought us from Bering Strait were too great a burden for the local natives, still short of food supplies. I tried to persuade drivers from Dezhnev Cape to press on a little farther west, to the Etonnik Settlement, for example, but they refused. They considered their dogs in need of a good rest even before they would leave for home. They were also afraid of the hunger rumored as prevailing along the shore west of North Cape. At North Cape I could find only one owner of a dog team ready to help us until we reached the Etonnik settlement.

There was nothing for me to do but to drive with our own dogs to Shelagski Cape, and in case of emergency to proceed toward the Koluima River, sending dogs from there for Weber. I would have liked to send Weber ahead and myself wait at North Cape, but I could not because his instruments made Weber's load much heavier than mine, and, besides, he needed a driver and I did not. Furthermore, I did not know what the trouble was and was not sure that Weber would be able to find the best way out of the difficulties.

On January tenth Berejnov and I left North Cape. Our third companion was a Chukcha from Koliuchin Island. He traveled with only four dogs and without any load. His long trip was undertaken in the hope of meeting Koluima people and buying from them several dogs. We gave him several of our dogs and in this way made up three *nartas* with heavy loads, for besides our former baggage we took with us the *chum* which we had left at North Cape on our way eastward. The same Koliuchin Chukcha, returning from Shelagski Cape, was to convey to Weber all information and instructions.

We were traveling rather slowly, taking care of our dogs, as we did not know how long we would have to use them. Once we made a stop for a day with a rich Chukcha, where we expected to find plenty of food. Other stops were forced by blizzards, which again were frequent. On the road we were joined by a fourth companion, who was also traveling westward in the hope of buying several dogs. He took a part of our load and we could now travel a little faster.

At the Etonnik settlement we stopped for the night with the family suffering from the itch. The same scratching as that of more than two months past greeted us from all corners. The *polog*, however, was not so overcrowded and our candle burned without flickering. The danger of infection was also less. The Chukchi in our party understood the contagious character of the sickness and told us about its spreading from this *yeranga*. Here I succeeded in renting two dog teams which were to go to North Cape and help Weber move to the Etonnik settlement.

At the Echunnin settlement I learned with astonishment that the teams from Koluima River had actually arrived at Shelagski Cape; but the drivers did not want to wait for us and left for home. I did not find Kozhevnicov at Shelagski Cape either. In a letter, Kozhevnicov gave me an exact report on all happenings. He had stayed at the settlement over a month. The situation had been desperate, the shortage of food had been so extreme that the people nearly starved. Kozhevnicov's supplies were also very limited, but he shared them with the population of the *yeranga* in the *polog* of which he was a guest. His discomfort had been aggravated by the itch which he had contracted at the Etonnik settlement and which, without any medical attention, had become worse.

On December twenty-ninth dogs hired for us at a price of a hundred rubles for a *narta* had arrived from the Koluima River, the "Rescue Expedition" as the whole enterprise was proudly called at Sredne-Koluimsk. All contracts had been made by the administration, and again in the same bureaucratic way that we had witnessed and from which we had suffered in the spring. One provision of the contract was particularly strange; the drivers were obliged to wait for us at the Shelagski Cape for two weeks, after which they had the right to return home. Kozhevnicov explained the situation, telling them that we were waiting for dogs at North Cape. During a whole week he tried to persuade them to drive eastward to help us. Realizing that the situation was helpless, he left for Koluima to begin all over again. The "rescuers" stayed a week more and turned back home.

The administration was certainly not responsible for the behavior of the contractors at the Cape, but I wondered many times whether it was not possible to send over more responsible people than those. My order to them was to bring as much dog food as it would be possible to carry. They brought only the small amount sufficient for the passage to Shelagski Cape, arriving there without even a bite of food. Immediately they found our cache of horse meat and disposed of it as though it were their own property, in spite of the protests of Kozhevnicov. The natives, by the way, had not touched those meat supplies at all. The rescuers also brought more dogs than they needed, and immediately after arriving sold about twenty-five—two full teams—to the natives. Some provisions I had ordered were sent but were mostly consumed by the contractors and Berejnov, and I found very little left for us.

Conditions at the Shelagski settlement at the time of our arrival were not better, but worse than described by Kozhevnicov. Seal hunting, the main source of meat in winter, was very poor. Real famine was imminent and as a matter of fact was avoided only by chance. At the time of our arrival it was learned that some Reindeer

Chukchi were staying at a place about three or four days' drive inland. All the men of the settlement immediately decided to start on an expedition after the reindeer meat. Under such conditions we could not stay at Shelagski waiting for Weber and new rescuers from Koluima, especially as we had to feed about thirty dogs. But to leave for Koluima we had to collect an amount of food sufficient for seven to ten days. Fortunately, during our trip we bought food wherever we could find it. Fish which was brought for us we turned over to the dogs. The last resources were discarded horse heads. With knives we cut out all soft parts, tongues and brains, and so collected meat for two or three days more. For several days we worked hard on preparations for our journey. We lost one day because of a snow storm.

On leaving for Koluima our rescuers had left at Shelagski a dog team, the property of Rumyanzev, which he ordered for his own use. Not knowing at that time that it would be a source of new troubles for me, I sent Rumyanzev's *narta* eastward to meet our companions.

Not until the last day of January, late in the afternoon, were we able to leave Shelagski Cape. Our first stop was made at nearby Rautan Island, where, we were told, two natives lived. We found them dwelling in the smallest *polog* I have ever seen. The surface of the floor was scarcely larger than a full-sized bed, and when I sat upright my head touched the ceiling. In some way or other we found room to stretch out, with Berejnov sleeping close to the young couple. They did not object to our intrusion but showed their hospitality as best they could. With real pleasure the next morning I gave them a few small presents, which were greatly appreciated. I did not try to find out what they were doing on that isolated island. Perhaps it was only a happy honeymoon trip.

Between Rautan Island and the Sukharnoye settlement we had neither regular settlers nor honeymooners. The region was a desert and we had to rely on our own resources. Although our dogs were in bad condition, with good weather we might expect to cover the distance in about a week; and we were sure that we had dog food and provisions for that length of time. But if we ran into the violent storms, gales, and heavy snowfall common there, lasting perhaps for days, the fresh, soft snow would spoil the road and we and our dogs would starve. For the time being the road was hard almost everywhere, and our dogs, exhausted though they were, could move at good speed on level ground. We had to help them, however, at every small elevation and at every patch of soft snow. We could easily imagine what our travel would be like after a blizzard or even a light snowfall. Before starting from Cape Shelagski, I had pointed out to Berejnov what might befall us if the weather should change for the worse. Fortunately, I found in him sufficient adventurous spirit to take the risk.

We carried a small box-shaped tent of cotton cloth which our workmen had used the previous summer. We had also a sleeping bag made of reindeer skins, cut in the simplest fashion, which covered legs and body to the breast. A fur blanket covered the upper part of the body. Underneath the sleeping bag, on the snow, we spread a reindeer skin. As we could not strip and dry our clothes at night, sleeping was not so comfortable, at least at the beginning. After a few days our underwear was always damp, making it particularly unpleasant when we crawled together into the cold sleeping bag. The task of heating our sleeping paraphernalia with the warmth of our bodies would take at least half an hour, then our shivering would cease and we would fall asleep and lie as if dead.

Crossing Chaun Bay we took another chance. The usual winter road lies south of Aion Island and across Karchuik Peninsula. I wanted to see the northern side of Aion Island, so we selected the northern route, although it was a little longer than the southern one. We passed the island safely, realizing all the while that, during a blizzard, travel over the northern part of the island would be extremely dangerous. The comparatively high shores of Aion Island were clearly visible, but travel near the shores was nearly impossible. The island was bordered with an irregular belt of shoals with plenty of driftwood, but the shoal belt was broken up by areas of clear ice marking the somewhat deep water. Within those clear ice areas there would suddenly appear large shoals with accumulations of driftwood, around which we had to detour. It was very difficult to keep to the right course unless we could see the high coast all the time. The first night in camp, far north of the shore but with plenty of driftwood around, I traced on the ice the direction for the next day's travel. Early in the morning I found our bearings by the stars, and in that way we were able to travel two or three hours before dawn, when we could see the coast again. During a blizzard or fog such reckoning would no longer be possible, and it would be very easy to become lost. In summer the shores of the island were similar to those on the western side of Karchuik Peninsula, which had been the despair of Kozhevnicov during the previous summer.

Near the Bolshaya River we met two *nartas* that had been sent for the expedition. Drivers told me that two more *nartas* followed. These drivers were better instructed and were ready to drive eastward as far as necessary. The meeting gave me great comfort. There was now no reason to worry about Weber and Rumyanzev.

The night before we reached the Sukharnoye settlement. We gave our dogs the last of the food, and for ourselves we had only a large can of corned beef and a few pounds of rice. We realized that corned beef was a good enough appetizer, but that it could not be used as a staple food. We could not eat it in amounts which I considered sufficient, but perhaps our mistake was that, desiring a warm meal, we had tried to make soup out of corned beef and rice.

On the ninth day after we left Shelagski, the eighth of February, we arrived at Sukharnoye, where we were met by Berejnov's relatives, who showed us every hospitality. They had seen us approaching a long distance away and took us for Chukchi, but had not understood why natives drove so slowly. We were considered very lucky in not encountering even a slight snow storm for nine days. We listened to all the excited exclamations, drank innumerable glasses of tea, and ate frozen fish, all the while growing more and more drowsy. What a pleasure to sleep undressed in a warm bed without worries for the next day!

The next morning I noticed that my fingers were swollen. It was childish, but I considered it a certain proof of weakness and tried not to expose my hands to the other people. Suddenly Berejnov said: "What a strong fellow I should be if I should have forever such thick fingers!" His fingers were swollen even more than mine, and he was a strong young fellow accustomed to conditions of such travel as ours.

18

RETURN TO ST. PETERSBURG

FROM Sukharnoye to the Pokhodsk village we drove with dogs now well fed and rested, but with both drivers struggling against drowsiness. At Pokhodsk I said good-by to Berejnov, with whom I had become good friends, particularly during the last part of our trip when we shared everything, including the sleeping bag. I sold Berejnov the dogs confiscated from Kuropachka, but for a price which made the sale something like a farewell present. From Pokhodsk I traveled as a passenger, changing dogs and drivers at every station. On February eighteenth, I arrived at Sredne-Koluimsk. Kozhevnicov, looking thinner and much older, met me on the shore with tears in his eyes. With the aid of the doctor who was in charge of the leprosery, he had just rid himself of the itch he had contracted at Etonnik. He told me about it immediately with a feeling of great relief, and at the same time with some bitterness toward the doctor who had not even tried to conceal his nausea while treating my sick friend. It was not surprising that this man of medicine never visited his lepers.

All of our former friends were glad to see us, and on

the day of my arrival I was invited to a party where we stayed well after midnight. During the long winter when people have no particular work to do and are confined to their houses, such parties become almost a nightly event. Kozhevnicov, in the capacity of guest of honor, had not missed one of them during his long wait for me. The next day we decided to have a Russian bath, in my case to scrub off two months' accumulation of dirt. The oven of the Russian bath is filled up with many pebbles which have been heated by a wood fire. When the pebbles are hot enough, the fire is stopped and the chimney closed, to prevent a draft and quick cooling. Water thrown on the pebbles fills the room with hot vapors in which one feels particularly comfortable.

At a fixed time, the bath was ready for use. Ours was a small shack of two rooms, one for undressing, the other for washing. The oven with heated pebbles was in the second room, which could be made as hot as one desired; in spite of a heap of snow and ice in one corner, the room was hot. I expected not only to wash but also to disinfect my body, for which I used green soap, a yellow, jelly-like substance yielding abundant lather. While washing off the green soap, I suddenly felt a throbbing in my temples, the familiar effect of carbon monoxide poisoning. Unfortunately, I could not wash off the green soap quickly enough, and by the time we had dressed ourselves and jumped out we were already quite dizzy. I lay down on a large pile of snow and my labored gasping breath resembled that of a fish pulled out of water. When I was chilled enough, I went to visit some friends nearby. The ever-ready samovar was there, with different palatable attractions. Kozhevnicov was there already, leaning against the table and not thinking about anything but his terrific headache. Half-frozen, I went to bed and stayed for two or three hours. We left after a while without having paid any attention to the prepared repast, to the great disappointment of our hostess as well as to ourselves. The next day, probably owing to my heroic treatment, I was all right again, but Kozhevnicov stayed in bed all day with a violent headache.

We had been entertained so generously everywhere in the town that we decided to give our own farewell party. Before anything definite was arranged, the rumor of the coming entertainment spread, and everybody was interested in whether he or she would receive an invitation. The number of invitations was limited only by the size of our house. We were lodged in the largest place in town, but there was not enough room to invite everybody. The invitations were therefore addressed very carefully by Kozhevnicov, who knew better than I the local society. He was assisted by our landlord, who took particular care not to bring together those who would not mix well. The next serious question concerned refreshments. We were unable to offer what we wanted to, having only what we could find at the stores. The excitement among the beauties of the town was indescribable. New toilets were made, old ones refreshed, and borrowing went on as well. I remembered an amusing story told by Baron Wrangel, who had been at Sredne-Koluimsk about a hundred years before our expedition. At a certain moment during a party like ours, all the girls left the room, appearing a few minutes later in new dresses. Such a change of attire was repeated several times. Poor creatures—not often having an opportunity to display their toilets, they had invented a method to satisfy their vanity! Fortunately for fathers and husbands, Wrangel's book is practically unknown to women of the civilized countries of Europe and America, and the invention of the Sredne-Koluimsk women has not met, therefore, with such popularity as it undoubtedly deserves.

Men did not show any excitement or even seem to care about their appearance. As usually accepted there, they appeared in their everyday clothes. But entertained they had to be, and their favorite game—cards. One table was prepared for gamblers ready to try their luck in a hazardous game called *shtoss*, or bank. Fortunes passed through several hands in a very short time in that game. Tables for the Russian *vint*, a card game very similar to bridge, were prepared for people who disliked taking great chances. For matrons, there were tables of *preference*, another Russian card game more innocent even than *vint*. For young people there were dances and Russian games. There was much singing and dancing in those games. Everyone had plenty of opportunity to show his wit, his presence of mind, to perform for this or that individual of the opposite sex. It was a good party, a great success! The house was filled to capacity and the fun was still going on long after midnight. Kozhevnicov, stimulated a bit by the bank table, was so moved by his first success that the next morning he was short a few hundred rubles. In dancing and gaming we often took part, very effectively helped by a local Russian priest who was the soul of the party. I hope he was a good priest as well. During the games we received hearty kisses from all the local beauties, not because we were particularly attractive to them but because we were the hosts and St. Petersburg people.

When I returned to Sredne-Koluimsk, I realized that we were short of funds and if we paid all the bills we could not cover the expenses of our trip to Yakutsk, where we could get money from St. Petersburg. We could order money from Sredne-Koluimsk, but that would require more than a month of waiting because of the lack of telegraphic connections between Sredne-Koluimsk and Yakutsk at that time. I asked the local Ispravnik to lend us a few hundred rubles, but he had only nine hundred rubles in his cash box and was not expecting to obtain additional funds soon. He advised me to apply for a loan from a local merchant, whom I visited the next day. The merchant asked only how much we needed. When I told him "about two thousand rubles," he left the room, and returned a few minutes later with twenty one-hundred-ruble bills. Probably he was not the only one in that miserable town who had secreted a big sum of money somewhere under his bed. He was so eager to show his good will in helping us in our financial difficulties that I could hardly persuade him to take a receipt from me.

We left Sredne-Koluimsk on February twenty-fourth in two covered *nartas*. For us that trip was a real rest, although we were traveling day and night, stopping only to change reindeer or horses and take food. In the daytime, as long as there was light and we were not sleeping, we read different novels, a great store of which we had taken from Sredne-Koluimsk. To the occasional observer we presented the comic picture of readers wrapped in furs holding a book in big fur gloves. Not for everyone would such a trip be so comfortable as it was for us—the comfort was relative. The nurse from the leprosery, who was going to Yakutsk for her leave of absence and who traveled with us, arrived at Yakutsk very sick. She told us that she was full of admiration for our endurance.

Our trip was well prepared now. At every station we found stern orders from Governor Kraft reminding the stations of their duties and responsibilities to us. The station keepers were not only polite but tried to apologize for all the inconveniences of our trip last spring. Some of them told us naïvely they had not known who we were; others expressed their regret that I had had to walk so much.

Our trip was in general uneventful, perhaps with the exception of meeting the newly appointed Archbishop along the road, who was traveling to inspect the northern limits of his diocese. If I had not known that for a great many years he had served as head of the Russian Church in Alaska, I should have deduced from his behavior that he had been living among foreigners. When we approached each other, struggling in our heavy fur coats in a deep snow, I was ready, following the custom of the Russian Church, to ask him for his benediction. He grasped my hand and shook it heartily. He was a very pleasing, appealing man and I regretted very much that we met each other on the road, not at a station.

We arrived at Yakutsk on March eleventh, two weeks after we had left Sredne-Koluimsk. On the eve of our coming Governor Kraft left the city for the town of Viluisk. The rumor was that he wished to avoid meeting me, but I do not think it was because of animosity. Perhaps he was embarrassed about all the unnecessary trouble through which the expedition had passed because of the stupidity and negligence of his subordinates, and also because of his absence from Yakutsk in the spring of 1909. I am sure he felt responsible for many of our troubles and that a meeting would have been unpleasant for both of us.

The vice-governor, whom I had kept in my memory as a great liar, was also out of the city. The acting governor was some rather small official with whom we transacted all our official business.

At Yakutsk it was necessary to wait for money from St. Petersburg to pay our loan at Sredne-Koluimsk, to settle some bills at Yakutsk, to send and receive a number of telegrams, and to pack and mail whatever we wished to forward from there.

I was a little surprised at the style of the telegrams we received from St. Petersburg. I felt that the news of our arrival at Yakutsk was received in an unusually jubilant manner for which I saw no reason, but later on I learned that even outside of Russia there was much talk about our dangerous situation. My family were living at that time in Switzerland, and my wife had been seriously alarmed several times when she learned that something had happened to the expedition. My wife was so much troubled by the rumors, the falsity of which was sufficiently proved by their renewal, that she did not credit the news of my arriving at Yakutsk. To a friend, one of the members of the Russian Academy of Sciences who congratulated her upon my return, she answered that she would believe in my coming only when she saw me.

Also, on the eve of our departure from Yakutsk, I received from Sredne-Koluimsk a letter which told me that Weber, without waiting for dogs, had moved from North Cape to Dezhnev Cape with the same Chukchi who had brought us from Bering Strait. He had not waited for the Chukcha from Koluichin Island, who according to our agreement was to carry him all information and instructions. So the work Kozhevnicov and I had done in sending the second party of dogs, as well as all the expense involved, went for nothing. I was quite sure that it was Rumyanzev who was responsible for such a sudden decision by Weber, and indirectly I, too, was at fault, because I had sent Rumyanzev his dogs from Shelagski Cape. As soon as Rumyanzev had an opportunity for independent movement, he probably represented to Weber all the conditions of the return journey in such a way that Weber lost his nerve, and turned back at the time when the dogs intended for him were already approaching North Cape. Rumyanzev apparently got them, because he brought back all the baggage of the expedition which Weber had not taken along. At Yakutsk I also received a letter from Weber, sent with Rumyanzev. We could not help but think that Weber himself could very well have overtaken us at Yakutsk. The story gave me several unpleasant moments later when some good friends tried to twist the situation to imply that I had abandoned Weber at North Cape. I corresponded with his relatives in Switzerland and had explanations to make to friends of his family in St. Petersburg. With documents in my hands, I was able to prove to the satisfaction of those concerned that the separation at North Cape was unavoidable. The following June I received a telegram from Weber from Dezhnev Cape via Nome, and in August he returned to St. Petersburg by way of Vladivostok.

We left Yakutsk on March twenty-first. The trip to Irkutsk was an exact repetition of the experience of the previous year, even to such a detail as the lack of snow between the last station and Irkutsk. We sold our sledge and again took a mail wheel carriage. We had only a little baggage, and the sledge was filled with straw. We ordered the straw taken out and examined carefully, as it was easy to lose something in it during a long trip. "I see," said one of the men present, "you have come a long way. The straw is not ours, it is very short."

On April sixteenth we arrived in St. Petersburg, thirteen months after our departure. In addition to a number of special reports to different officials and organizations interested in the question of northern communication, I read a number of papers before different scientific and technical societies interested in geography, geology, navigation, and related matters. Everywhere the most important question concerned the possibility of commercial sea travel into the embouchure of the Koluima River. During our trip I saw so much open sea along the coast that I was quite positive in my answers, and able to answer any argument against the project, so we

were elated over the decision of the Russian Free Fleet
to send, in 1911, the steamer "*Koluima*" under command
of Admiral Troyan into the Koluima River. The
Koluima passed Bering Strait successfully and reached
the Koluima River, the same summer returning to
Vladivostok. From a commercial point of view the trip
was not a success, because the cargo was very small and
the price of transportation accordingly very high. But
nobody expected to make money with the experiment.
Since then steamer travel into the Koluima River has
become virtually an annual event. Twice steamers were
bound by ice and remained for the winter in the Arctic,
without any bad effect. The new navigation that is
constantly growing in importance is undoubtedly the
direct result of our adventure and of the boldness of my
statements after our return.